THIS MORNING'S ⌐

© Redvers Brandling 1996

First published 1996 by
Nash Pollock Publishing
32 Warwick Street
Oxford OX4 1SX

10 9 8 7 6 5

Orders to:
64 Hallfield Road
Layerthorpe
York
YO3 7XQ

The author's moral right is asserted.

A catalogue record of this book is available from the British Library

ISBN 1 898255 11 3

Typeset in 11 on 13pt Galliard by Black Dog Design, Buckingham
Cover illustration by Clare Mattey
Printed in Great Britain by T. J. International Ltd, Padstow, Cornwall

THIS MORNING'S STORY

100 Assemblies for Primary Schools

Redvers Brandling

Nash Pollock Publishing

Acknowledgements

I am as always grateful to former staff and children of Dewhurst St Mary School, Cheshunt. For so many years they were a receptive audience for assemblies, and a source of both inspiration and information with their own presentations.

I am grateful to David Morgan who told me the story 'The discovery'. 'Accident' first appeared in another form in *It Makes You Think* published by Edward Arnold; and 'A Fair Exchange' and 'The Last Tree' first appeared in *Christmas in the Primary School*, published by Ward Lock Educational. Different versions of 'The traveller alone', 'That's what we'll do', and 'Let's celebrate' first appeared in *Contact: Christian Assemblies for Primary Schools* (Blackwell).

The School Curriculum and Assessment Authority's *Model Syllabuses for Religious Education Document* (1994) has proved an invaluable source, particularly for multi-cultural reference. It could be recommended to all teachers.

It should also be mentioned that some of the stories in this book have been used and re-adapted several times in assemblies. In consequence their original sources are not remembered and if this has unwittingly caused the infringement of copyright, the author apologises and will correct the omission in future editions if notified.

Contents

II True stories

III Christian stories

IV Stories from other religions and cultures

V Christmas stories

VI Stories for other festive occasions

Introduction

The legal requirements regarding assemblies, and the genuine desire of most primary school heads and teachers to make such occasions significant, interesting and worthwhile, means that the demand for useful, practical assembly books never ends.

The School Curriculum and Assessment Authority's detailed 1994 publication on Religious Education should have surprised nobody with its comments that RE should help pupils to: 'acquire and develop knowledge and understanding of Christian beliefs and other principal religions ... develop an understanding of the influence of beliefs, values, traditions ... enhance their own spiritual, moral, cultural and social development ... develop a positive attitude towards other people... '

These factors, along with others such as wonder, admiration, awe and concern are the bases of good assemblies.

This book, which is aimed for primary/middle/lower secondary use, seeks to provide a detailed compendium of material from which assembly presenters can draw. There are one hundred stories for assembly and these are divided into six sections: Tales past and present, True stories, Christian stories, Stories from other religions and cultures, Christmas Stories, and Stories for other festive occasions.

Following each assembly story there is some comment to help expand the presentation. This comment includes suggestions for immediate and longer term follow up work, useful addresses where relevant, notes on words, phrases, events and quotations which would help to enhance and strengthen the presenter's background knowledge. It also includes extra thematic suggestions.

I

Tales past and present

1
Think before you speak

There is a quotation in the Bible which says: A fool rushes into a house, while a man of experience hangs back politely (Ecclesiasticus 22:22). Sometimes we are too keen to speak quickly and without thought ....

Dean was in a very bad mood. It was Saturday morning and he was going to the judo club on his bike – at least he thought he was until he found his bike had a puncture. So he'd had to walk all the way there and all the way back. Dean was in a very bad mood.

"Well, at least Mum'll have the dinner ready," thought Dean, as he turned the corner to the street where he lived. Soon he reached his house and then, looking down past the side of it into the back garden he saw his brother Shane – with his bike!

Dean was furious. He broke into a run, yelling as he went. "Hey, what are you doing with my bike? Don't you know it's got a puncture?"

Shane looked up, startled. "Yeah, course I do. Mum told me. I've just been to the shops and got a repair outfit. I was going to mend it for you as a surprise."

"Oh," said Dean in a small voice. He wished he hadn't been in such a hurry to accuse his brother.

Of course it is not only children who speak quickly and harshly without thinking. Adults do it too and there is an old story which shows this.

A man had died, and he was at the Gates of Heaven talking over his life with St Peter.

"Well, let's have a look at your journey through life," said Peter.

So the two of them looked at a chart of the man's life. All through it were the man's footprints, and another set of footprints alongside his – for most of the way.

"There are your footprints through life," said Peter.

"And there are God's walking with mine?" queried the man.

"Yes, that's right."

"But ... just a minute," went on the man. "Look at these gaps when there are only my footprints."

"Yes."

"Well," said the man, his voice getting more angry as he spoke, "if God was supposed to be beside me through life the missing footprints show that this wasn't the case – and what's more there are only one set of footprints at the most difficult, worrying and distressing parts of my life!"

"Yes, that's right," replied St. Peter. "They're God's. You see he was carrying you then."

Notes

Follow up themes: thinking before we speak; questions; words which help.

The following poem could be used as a prayer to end this service:

A word here
A word there
A word chosen
With some care.
A kind word
A thoughtful word ...
Thanks
Well done
Welcome
Please
A word chosen
With some care
Is a gift
For all to share.

Geoffrey Simpson

2
The missing axe

An honest man is sometimes rewarded more than he expects. A dishonest man sometimes loses all he had to start with.

Jacob was a poor woodcutter. His most precious possession was his axe. Without this he could not chop wood and therefore could not make enough to live on. One day he was chopping a log when his axe hit a big knot in the wood, flew out of his hands and sank beneath the surface of the fast flowing river beside which he was working.

"My axe!" groaned Jacob. "My axe – it's gone! How can I live without my axe?"

So saying, the poor man sat down on the log and buried his face in his hands. To his astonishment he suddenly felt a hand on his shoulder, and, opening his eyes, he saw a strange figure in front of his.

"My friend," said the figure. "I saw what happened. Is this your axe?"

Jacob looked at the axe in the stranger's hand. It was made of solid gold.

"No ..." he blurted out. "Thank you ... but I'm afraid it's not my axe."

The stranger put the gold axe on the ground and, opening his hands caught another axe which flew up out of the river. It was made of solid silver!

"What about this axe?"

"Thank you again for your help," gasped Jacob, "but I'm afraid that's not my axe either."

Once again the stranger put the axe on the ground and, opening his hands, caught the third axe which flew out of the river. This time Jacob recognised the worn old tool which he had used for so many years.

"Yes!" he cried. "Oh thank you sir – that's my axe!"

"So," said the mysterious stranger, "as you are such an honest man you may keep both the gold and the silver axes as well."

And so Jacob became better off than he had ever been in his life. A few days later he was telling Anton, his neighbour, of his good fortune. Now Anton was a jealous, sly man and as Jacob talked he was already working out how he could get rich too.

The next morning he set off to chop wood in the same spot by the fast flowing river. As he chopped he pretended to lose his grip on his axe, which flew into the water.

Slumping miserably onto a log as Jacob had done, he covered his eyes and ... yes, when he opened them, there stood the mysterious figure.

"I saw your misfortune," said the stranger. "Is this the axe you lost?" So saying he showed Anton a magnificent gold axe.

As soon as he saw it, Anton's greed made him forget his plans and he blurted out hurriedly, "Yes, yes that's my axe – let me have it."

"You're lying," said the stranger, "and because of that you will not have it, nor will you find the axe you lost." With that he disappeared as mysteriously as he had arrived.

(Based on an Aesop's fable)

Notes

Follow up themes: honesty, hardship, wise counsel.

This is one of those very simple, yet fascinating stories, which makes 'instant drama' with primary children a fruitful and enjoyable activity. As such it could be presented in dramatic form in assembly with practically no preparation.

Concluding prayer

Let us think this morning about how easy it is to say something is ours when it isn't. Let us pray that we can always be honest and never make claims which we will later regret. Amen.

3
Surprise, surprise

Have you ever acted unkindly to someone who is old?

Mrs Johns lived in an end house on the way to our school. She was a really, really old widow and when we saw her struggling in her garden there was a lot of pushing and shoving and giggling.

"Watch out for the bearded lady," sniggered Ella. Mrs Johns had some wispy hairs round her chin. "Wish I had my long johns on," spluttered Cosmo. Mrs Johns was very tall.

All in all she used to give us a lot of laughs on our way to and from school. But, no matter how we joked and poked fun, she never seemed to lose her temper. Instead, she always seemed to be staring off into space as if we weren't there.

One day the headmaster asked my mum if she'd give out some notices about the school fête. She decided to do this after school one day and Ella and I went along with her.

One of the last houses she went to was Number 47, next door to Mrs Johns'.

"Come on in," insisted the lady who owned the house. "Just have a seat in the front room while I get some change."

We did this, and almost immediately we were aware of the sound of piano music through the wall from the house next door.

"Long Johns has got the radio turned up a bit," whispered Ella behind a cupped hand.

"Oh, that's not the radio," said the lady of the house who had just come back into the room and heard the last part of Ella's whisper. "That's Mrs Johns playing the piano."

We all stopped what we were doing for a minute and listened to the sweeping music coming through the wall. It was breathtakingly fast, full of rippling notes and tremendously exciting.

"Good isn't she?" smiled the hostess.

A couple of minutes later we were outside Mrs Johns house. Quite a long time after Mum had rung the doorbell the door opened slowly and Mrs Johns stood there. The grey wisps of hair on her chin were very noticeable, and she was tall. She was leaning on a stick and seemed out of breath.

"I'm sorry to disturb you, but ..."

Mum went on to tell her about the fête and raffle tickets and so on. When she'd finished Mrs Johns reached back to a shelf beside the door and took down a well worn purse. She paid Mum for the raffle tickets and was just turning away when Ella blurted out, "Can we listen to you play the piano?"

The old lady turned back to us. "Aren't you one of those girls I sometimes see when I'm trying to do my garden?"

I watched the blush creep up Ella's neck, reach her ears and then spread to her face. "Well I am ... but I don't ... I mean ..."

Ella's embarrassment was eased when Mrs Johns interrupted. "Yes I thought you were – and of course you can hear me play. Come on in."

We trooped into the house after the old lady. Everything looked neat and well polished but old – until we saw the piano. It was a modern electric one with various little knobs ranged along the edge of the keyboard. The old lady sat down in front of it.

"What would you like me to play?"

Mum was there in a flash. "My husband and I had a lovely holiday once and the band where we were was always playing 'Blue Moon ...'

Before she could go any further Mrs Johns' hands were caressing the keyboard with darting, flickering fingers. The vibrant rhythm of the music filled the room and the old lady's body seemed to shed its stiffness as she swayed in tempo.

Well, we were in there for half an hour. Mum was quite carried away. She asked for one or two more of her favourites, and Mrs Johns laughingly played something which she said was popular when she was about our age – 'Run Rabbit Run' it was called.

When Ella muttered something about pop and the charts Mrs Johns immediately had Ella and me snapping our fingers to some of our favourites.

Finally Mum asked a question. "I'm sure you're quite busy, Mrs Johns ... but the school is having a fête on Saturday afternoon and I'm sure it would be hugely popular if you could come along and play ... and do requests ... and ..."

Mrs Johns gave a smile that lit up her whole face. "I'm not quite busy at all my dear, and I'd be delighted to come along and play. This piano comes to pieces very easily so if somebody could come and carry it to the school for me ..."

Well, you've guessed it. Mrs Johns was the star of the school fête. She played for two hours non-stop, never looked at a piece of music and answered everybody's requests for favourite pieces.

It's a funny thing, you know, but I never hear anybody calling her 'the bearded lady' or 'Long Johns' anymore.

Notes

Follow up themes: old age; understanding; tolerance; appearances; talents.

A useful Bible reading here is:

"Do not overrate one man for his good looks or be repelled by another man's appearance. The bee is small among the winged creatures, yet her perfume takes first place for sweetness." *Ecclesiasticus 11.2-3*

Prayer:

Dear God, Help us to value all people equally whether they be old, young, rich or poor. Help us to be kind and considerate at all times. Amen.

4
Lost and found

A purse full of money is lost. The owner tries to cheat the finder. What happens next?

Isaac put the twenty fifth gold coin into his large leather purse. When he had done this he tied the purse onto his belt because wherever he went he took it with him. Nobody loved money more than Isaac.

It was the worst thing in the world which could have happened, therefore, when exactly a week later after a long journey, Isaac reached down for his purse – and it was gone!

"Oh – misery, misery, me! My money ... all my money's gone. My money ... oh – oh – oh ."

After five minutes of wailing Isaac came to his senses. So he advertised his loss – and a reward for the finder. To his delight a man arrived at his house the next day.

"Good morning," said the man, whose name was Samuel. "I'm so glad you're in because I'm sure I've found your purse."

Isaac's eyes gleamed as he saw the purse in Samuel's hands. It was his! "Wonderful, wonderful," he said. "Now let me count the money and give you a good reward."

Very very slowly and carefully Isaac began to count the gold coins. As he felt each familiar shape and looked at the coin's gleam, he began to feel a sense of disappointment.

"Fancy having to give up one of my beautiful coins to a ... to a stranger," he thought to himself. "It's a terrible ... but ..."

Suddenly he had a thought! "Thank you again," he said quickly to the stranger. "I've counted the gold coins and there are twenty four here – so I see you have already taken your piece of gold which was the reward."

Now, of course Samuel had done no such thing and he was very angry that having brought the purse back to the owner he was being accused of taking money from it!

"I have taken nothing from the purse – and how dare you say I have! I care nothing for your reward, but I won't be accused in this way!"

So, within a few seconds the two men were arguing furiously – and eventually it was decided that only a judge could solve their differences.

"Each of you had better tell me his side of the story," said the judge when the two men stood before him.

The mean and dishonest Isaac spoke, and then Samuel told his tale. For a minute the judge sat still and silent, then after stroking his chin he gave his judgement in a loud, clear voice.

"Isaac, you have told us you lost a purse with twenty five gold crowns in it. Now Samuel had brought you one with tweny four gold crowns in it.

Obviously, therefore, it cannot be the same purse. So Samuel must keep the purse and the gold in it until its owner can be found. Meanwhile you, Isaac, must hope that someone finds your purse with the twenty five gold crowns in it."

Samuel thought this was the wisest judgement he had ever heard!

Adapted from an old Jewish folk tale

Notes

Follow up themes: Lost and found, honesty.

Concluding prayer:

Let us think this morning about honesty. We pray that, no matter what the temptation, we are always honest, fair and faithful. Amen.

5
The discovery

This is a story about two different points of view.

Ivan was a rich man. Everything he did was successful. He made more money, lived in bigger houses, had more servants. But he wasn't happy.

"I don't know what it is ," he thought, "nothing seems to satisfy me. I wonder …"

What he wondered was what he had heard other men talk about. "Selfishness never leads to contentment," one had said.

"Sharing – that's the answer," said another.

"You need God in your life," announced a third.

"Right," decided Ivan. "I'm going to find God."

So he made his preparations. He found a cave high up in the mountains alongside a narrow, lonely path. Into this cave he had his servants take food, clothes and a bed. Then, in the early days of spring he moved into it.

"Now," he thought, "I'm alone – nobody to bother me, nothing to do until I find God."

So Ivan lived in the cave. The days and weeks of spring and summer slipped by. He ate well, slept in his comfortable bed, strolled along the mountain path in the sunshine, and talked to the birds and himself. Gradually the warmer days gave way to autumn, and then the first chill of winter bit into the air in the cave.

"Six months I've been here," said Ivan to himself one day. "Six months and – nothing. I don't feel any different from how I felt before. Now I know it – there is no God."

Stepping out through a thin flurry of snow Ivan began to walk down the path to his home. When he arrived his servants noticed that he had not changed. "Come on," he snapped. "Back to that cave. I want everything brought out and returned here. Come on – hurry up!"

So Ivan and his servants went back to the cave and in a short while it was empty again. Looking into its gloomy depths Ivan was just about to follow his men when his foot caught a loose stone. Bending down he picked it up and went back into the cave. Just inside the entrance he used the stone to cut a message as deeply as he could into the wall.

GOD IS NOWHERE, he wrote.

The darkness and cold of winter deepened. Bitter winds swept over the mountain and ever freshly fallen snow made the path by the cave dangerous and difficult to walk along. Travellers were very few indeed.

Then, one freezing winter's night, a gaunt and ragged figure came edging along the path. In one hand he held a stick and with the other he tapped the mountainside. Oleg was blind and had to feel out his dangerous journey.

"If this wind and snow don't stop I'll never make it," he muttered to himself. "I can't rest up here and I'm getting too exhausted to go much further tonight. If only I could find somewhere to rest ... if ... only ..."

Just at that moment Oleg's tapping left hand began to flap in space. The mountainside was no longer there, and he quickly realised he had stumbled across the entrance to a cave. Falteringly he stepped inside and once again his hand began to trace a path along the wall. As it did so it came to the letters so recently and angrily cut there by Ivan.

"What's this?" whispered Oleg. Slowly his fingers crept over the letters.

G...O...D...I...S... "God is – it's a message," thought the weary traveller. His fingers read on.

N...O...W... "God is now ... I wonder what comes next?"

H...E...R...E... "Wonderful," cried Oleg aloud. "Wonderful. GOD IS NOW HERE. He is here with me and he has saved my life!"

Notes

Follow up themes: different viewpoints; happiness; searching.

A useful prayer in connection with this story is:

God, our Father, you can make all things new.
We commit ourselves to you: help us
To live for others since your love includes all men.

(Part of an Uppsala prayer used at the World Council of Churches)

6
Perfect?

In the market place in the city of Durham stands the statue of a man on a horse. It is a perfect piece of work – or is it?

John stood back and looked at the statue. Right in the middle of Durham's ancient market place the carving of the lord on his horse reared high and proud above the cobbles.

"Best work I've ever done," said John, whose sculpture it was. "In fact I'd even go so far as to say ... it's perfect."

"Hum."

"Aah."

"Y..es."

John was well liked and everybody admired his work, but ... perfect? That was why the gathering of his friends made polite noises but weren't sure.

"Perfect?" This was what another man said a little while later when he heard the story. He had been for many years a servant of the lord who had been carved in stone.

"I must know what my master looked like better than anyone else alive. I'll go and have a close look at the statue. I'm sure there must be a mistake in it somewhere."

So saying he journeyed to the market place, climbed onto the base of the statue, then the horse and for over an hour studied every detail of the statue's face. When he climbed down there was an interested crowd waiting to hear what he had to say.

"Well?"

The servant gave a short nod of his head.

"He's right. It's perfect."

After this there always seemed to be someone spending hours gazing at the statue. A well known horse dealer came and spent hours going over every detail of the carved animal's body.

"Perfect," was the only word he said when he had finished. A tailor examined the carved clothes on the statue. Could there be a button or button hole missing, was a fold wrongly shown, might a cuff be too short?

"No," said the tailor. "It's perfect."

And so the people of Durham took to boasting not only about their wonderful cathedral but also about their 'perfect' statue. Its fame spread far and wide.

One day a poor, wandering blind beggar arrived in the city. In his journeys all over the north he had heard a great deal about the perfect statue. Soon he found himself standing in the market place. There was the usual jostling crowd around.

"Ha, pity you can't see this statue," muttered a man standing next to the beggar. "People come from all over to look at it. It's perfect, you see – and famous for it."

"Oh I've heard of it all right," answered the beggar. "I'll never be able to see it – but do you think you could help me to feel it?"

"I don't see why not," replied the man. "Here Albert, give this chap a hand."

The two men lifted the blind beggar onto the base of the statue. Slowly he began to feel the huge carving.

The crowd around watched quietly. The beggar's sensitive fingers slid over the great muscles of the horse's neck. They fluttered along its mouth, stroked, stroked again, and stopped. For almost a minute they lay still.

There was a sudden restlessness in the crowd. "What's the matter?" called someone. "Why have you stopped there?" cried another.

The blind man turned his sightless eyes towards the crowd. "There's a mistake in this carving," he said quietly.

"What?"

"Rubbish!"

"Hundreds have looked – and nobody else has ever found one!"

Once again the blind man's fingers probed the horse's mouth. "This horse has been carved without a tongue," he said.

(Adapted from a Durham folk tale)

Notes

Follow up themes: modesty, handicaps, conceit.

The story goes that the beggar was never seen again after his dramatic discovery, and the sculptor, finding that his work was not perfect, killed himself.

This story contrasts well with the one about Persian carpet makers. They, believing that only Allah can make anything perfect, always make a small deliberate mistake in every carpet they produce.

The following prayer might be appropriate here:

Lord, Help us to do our best but to remember our good fortune in any gifts and skills we possess. Teach us to be modest and to value the talents of others. Amen.

7
Who can see that?

Whatever job we do, we should try to do it in the best possible way we can – the man in this story did.

"Let's go and see how Pheidias is getting on."
"Good idea."
"Phew, it's hot today though isn't it? I don't think I'd like to be working on a sculpture in this weather."
The men talking were Greeks and they lived in the city of Athens. They were all friends of a famous sculptor called Pheidias. He had been

given a special task by Pericles, the ruler of Greece. This task was to create beautiful buildings in Athens. Already he had supervised the building of the great Parthenon and he himself was carving a great statue inside this.

"I'm going to build a statue of Athene, the goddess of Athens," he had said to Pericles. "It is going to be made of ivory and gold and it will be twenty metres high."

Now the great statue was nearly finished and Pheidias' friends were going to visit the great man at work.

Strolling through the burning sunshine they soon reached the magnificent site of the Parthenon. There they saw the scaffolding surrounding the huge statue of the goddess. High up at the top, chipping away, was Pheidias. The friends began to climb up the scaffolding.

The sculptor saw them climbing up. "Hello," he called, "I'm glad you could spare the time to come and see me."

"I was going to say it's a pleasure, but it's very hot up here," said one of the friends. "What are you doing?" asked another.

"Ah well, I'm just carving a strand of hair on top of Athene's head," explained Pheidias.

"You're what?" queried the first friend. "Carving a strand of hair on top of her head, but ..."

"But," interrupted another, "when this scaffolding is taken away nobody will possibly be able to even see the top of the head."

"That's right," went on the first friend. "You're wasting your time – nobody will be able to see whether you've done this work or not."

"You're wrong there," retorted Pheidias. "The gods will be able to see."

Notes

Follow up themes: doing one's best; talents; honesty.

The time of this story is nearly five hundred years before the birth of Christ.

The Bible reading chosen for this morning's prayer is one which can be used again in conjunction with any stories of 'worthy' men or women.

"The memory of him will not die but will live on from generation to generation; the nations will talk of his wisdom, and his praises will be sung in the assembly. If he lives long, he will leave a name in a thousand, and if he goes to his rest his reputation is secure."

Ecclesiasticus 39:9-11

8
It's cold outside

All of us have been tempted at some time in our lives to do something we know we shouldn't. This morning's story is rather a strange one – but it was told to show people that once they let 'temptation' come in, then …

The two of them had been travelling all day in the hot desert sun. Man and camel were tired and thirsty. After they had both eaten and drunk the man, an Arab, pitched his tent for the night. The camel, he knew, was far better equipped to spend the night out in the open than he was.

The moon rose in the now cold, clear sky. Inside the tent the Arab curled in his sleeping bag. Suddenly, through the fastening of the tent, the camel forced its head.

"It's cold out here," it said. "Can I put my nose in?"

Now the Arab knew that the camel should stay outside but he was tired and he didn't want a fuss. "All right," he said, "just your nose."

Ten minutes later the Arab was fast asleep when the camel spoke again. "I'm still cold. Can I put my head in?"

"Wh – what," muttered the Arab dazedly. "Oh … oh all right then." Back he went to sleep.

The next time he was awakened, the camel asked to put its neck in … and the next time its front legs … and the next time its hump.

Finally, the whole camel was in the tent and the Arab was crammed right up beside the side of the tent.

"Hey," said the Arab, wide awake now, "there's no room for me in here."

"Why don't you go outside then?" smirked the camel.

There was a pause.

"Oh, if only I hadn't let him put his nose in," thought the man.

(Adapted from an old Eastern fable.)

Notes

Follow up themes: "It won't matter just this once"; rules; self discipline.

Prayer:
Dear God, Please give us the strength and wisdom to avoid doing things we know we should not do. Help us to resist all dishonesty and cheating. Amen.

9
The gold coin

John Duck has been called 'the Dick Whittington of Durham'. 'Never give up' was his motto – and many people were glad of it!

"Clear off, we don't want you here."
"Sorry – I've got no work for you. Try another town."
Time and again young John Duck heard the same message. He had come to the city of Durham in search of work, but could find nothing. One day, disappointed and discouraged, he was wandering along one of the city's river banks.
"I'm prepared to work really hard if only somebody would give me a chance," he sighed to himself, "but ..."
Just then the young man noticed a raven circling above his head. It had something in its mouth.
"Lucky you," John called to the bird, "I could do with something to eat too."
No sooner had he spoken however than what he thought was a piece

of food fell from the raven's mouth and landed at his feet. John bent down and found, to his astonishment, that it was a gold coin.

"Fantastic!" he cried. "I've actually got some money. What a meal I can get with this ... but maybe I can put it to better use."

John spoke the last words to himself as he saw a tired, harassed looking man heading towards him, driving two cows. The man got nearer.

"I'm sick and tired of these two awkward creatures," the man grumbled. "I'm taking them to market but I'm so fed up with them I'd sell them now to anybody who would give me a fair price."

"I'll buy them," replied John, at once.

"What have you got?" asked the man, suddenly more interested.

John offered the man the gold coin and in a minute the deal was done. He knew he had got a bargain and could hardly wait to get the cows to market himself. Sure enough, once he had done so he sold them for a handsome profit.

That was just the change of luck John Duck had needed. From this first deal he worked hard, bought and sold and eventually became a very rich man. He never forgot less fortunate people, however, and gave help as much as he could. His reputation spread.

"If you want something done well, that John Duck's a good man to ask."

"Help – the best man to help you in this town is John Duck."

"A friend to all – that's what I say he is."

So, when it became time for a new mayor to be elected the people of Durham chose John Duck. Eventually, like the famous Dick Whittington of London, he became Sir John Duck and one of his last acts was to build a hospital at Lumley for sick and aged people who had not had his good fortune.

(Adapted from a Durham fold tale)

Notes

Follow up themes: determination; thought for others; poverty; making the most of opportunities.

John Duck built himself a mansion in Durham's Silver Street. The street is still one of the city's busiest thoroughfares.

A thought for following up in assembly, and later in the classroom could be provoked by reference to the jingle:

"Great moments come to every man,
Some situations where he can,
Attain such fame that folks will claim
The very mention of his name."

The assembly might also be concluded with the following prayer/Bible reference:

"Be most careful how you conduct yourselves; like sensible men, not like simpletons." *Ephesians 5:15*

10

Qualities

If you look at the people standing near you in assembly you will already know some of their qualities. You might think John is kind, Julie is funny, Le Roy is hard working and so on. This story is about qualities ...

The teacher was having a discussion with the children in her class. They sat round in a large circle.

"Now," said Miss Waldie, "if you could choose the nicest thing you would want a person to say about you ... what would it be?"

There was no shortage of answers from the children.

"That I'm kind."

"Reliable."

"Thoughtful."

"Hard working."

"Cheerful."

"A good friend."

"Considerate to my parents."

"Truthful."

"Ah," interrupted Miss Waldie. "We've had the sort of answers you would expect. Sometimes however a good, and old, story helps us to remember and think more deeply about some of these things. Like this story ..."

The court was gathered together. It had come to make a judgement and it was a very strange sight indeed.

First of all, in the middle of the court was a huge pair of weighing scales. To one side of these stood a creature who had the body of a man, and the head of a dog. He spoke.

"Well, are we ready to begin? Can we make the judgement now?"

"Yes, Anubis, we can make the judgement now. All is ready."

The person who answered Anubis was even stranger to look at than he was. This was Thoth, who had the body of a man, and the head of a bird.

"Are you ready to write down the findings of the court, Thoth?"

"Yes," replied Thoth, whose job it was to record everything when the judgement was being made.

"In that case," went on Anubis, "bring her in."

The door of the strange court room opened and a woman came slowly in. She was wearing a white robe which covered her from head to foot.

Anubis nodded at her, but he did not smile or welcome her in any way.

"Do you know the rules?" he asked.

"I think so," replied the woman.

"Let me remind you of them then," continued Anubis, in a flat monotonous voice. "You have died and you have come here to the Court of Judgement to see what will happen to you now. Only your heart knows exactly how you have behaved all those years on earth – it cannot lie here."

The dog headed god then moved to one side and picked up two pans. He placed one on one side of the weighing balance, and the other on the other side.

He then carefully laid the woman's heart on one of the pans. Holding this still he snapped his fingers and commanded a nearby servant to put something else on the other pan.

The servant stepped forward and laid the lightest looking feather imaginable on the empty pan. Anubis still held tightly to the pan holding the heart.

"Now," he said to the woman, "here is the test. In the other pan is the Feather of Truth. Let's see how you fare in the weighing up process."

As he said this Anubis gently let go of the pan he was holding. For a few seconds the pans on the balance tilted slightly up and down. First the pan containing the heart dipped down, and then the one with the feather in did the same. After a few seconds however both became quite still – and perfectly balanced.

Anubis' dog face relaxed into a smile.

"Perfect," he exclaimed, "and congratulations. Your heart and the Feather of Truth balance perfectly. This means that you have lived a life full of truth, kindness and consideration. Your journey on from here is therefore quite straightforward – to the peace and beauty of the Fields of Yaru."

Notes

Follow up themes: good qualities; truth; making judgements.

All religions and cultures recognise the needs for good qualities in their followers, and in the writings of these there are exhortations and advice to this effect. The following are some examples:

"All that we are is the result of our thoughts." *(Buddha)*

"Be worthy of a reputation." *(Confucius)*

"The world is preserved by three things: truth, justice, peace." *(Jewish saying)*

"He is best loved who does most good to others." *(Islam)*

"Let us have real warm affection for one another as between brothers, and a willingness to let the other man have the credit. Share the happiness of those who are happy and the sorrow of those who are sad." *(From a letter from St. Paul to Christian in Rome.)*

A prayer to end the service could be:
Let us think this morning of the qualities we value most highly in others. Let us learn from these thoughts and become kinder and more considerate people as a result. Amen.

11
Pride goes before a fall

This old tale is a reminder that we should treat all people as we would like to be treated ourselves.

The horse carrying the knight in armour strode proudly along the road. Its equipment gleamed in the sunlight and the gloss of its coat was beautiful to see. It was on the way to join in the army's attack.

Coming along the road towards the magnificent horse was a scruffy, bedraggled donkey. Weighed down with a heavy load and panting loudly, the donkey looked with admiration at the other animal.

"What are you staring at?" snarled the horse. "Get out of the way, you miserable creature, or I'll trample you into the dirt."

Without replying the weary donkey stepped to the side of the road and horse and rider swept contemptuously past.

Weeks went by. During this time the donkey continued his daily work of carrying heavy loads and of being grateful when he was given good food. For the horse things were very different.

"Charge!" The word had rung in his ears as he galloped with colours flying towards some other horses on the other side of a field. The air had been full of the sound of shouts and pounding hooves and then suddenly ... he had felt a terrible pain in his side as a spear tore into his flesh. His rider hauled on his reins and he staggered back to the camp. The other voices had talked about him.

"Well, he was a good war horse – but he's useless now."

"Can't stay here I'm afraid, we'll have to get rid of him."

"Isn't there a farm back there where he could be sent to work?"

And so the weeks went by and the donkey was labouring up the familiar road at the usual time at the usual speed. Coming towards him he saw an enormous wagon. In front of it, straining to pull the load, was a horse. The horse was limping and his coat barely covered the jagged scar which ran down its side. Yet there was something familiar about the horse ...

"It can't be," thought the donkey. "It just can't be ... but it is!"

The sweating, limping horse drew alongside the donkey. He spoke.

"Any chance you could help me with these loads, friend?" he gasped pitifully.

(Adapted from Aesop)

Notes

Follow up themes: good manners, compassion, forgiveness.

Some other relevant Biblical quotations here are:
"If your brother wrongs you, reprove him; and if he repents forgive him. Even if he wrongs you seven times a day and comes back to you seven times saying 'I'm sorry,' you are to forgive him." *Luke 17:4.*

"Do not overrate one man for his good looks or be repelled by another man's appearance." *Ecclesiasticus 11:2*

"Happy is the man who had concern for those more helpless than himself." *Psalm 41:1*

One of these passages, adapted to meet the needs of the age group concerned could be used as the closing prayer.

12
All's well that ends well

Anansi stories are always entertaining in their own right. This one has a nice feeling of 'fairness' about it.

Anansi and Monkey were coming back from the market. As they walked through the forest they heard a strange voice.
"It's a bit like a roar," said Monkey.
"But it's a cry for help too!" replied Anansi.
As they got nearer to it the roar got louder and angrier – and more desperate.

"I think ... I think ... it's Tiger," mumbled Monkey nervously. "Let's keep right away."

"No, no we can't do that, perhaps he needs help," said Anansi. "Let's go and find out."

Tiger certainly did need help. He was trapped in a pit. The more he struggled the more he sank into the thick mess in the pit. His roars became more desperate.

"Ha, don't worry Tiger, we'll soon have you out," called Anansi reassuringly. "Here, catch this rope."

So saying he lowered something down to Tiger. It looked like a rope, but it was Monkey's tail!

"Hey ... but ... wait ..." spluttered Monkey.

It was too late. Tiger had already got a firm grip on the tail with his powerful teeth. Pulling, and scrambling with his front legs and claws, he dragged himself out of the pit. Then he got a pleasant surprise.

"It's not a rope at all," he said to himself. "It's Monkey's tail, and never did Monkey look more tasty. Dinner's right here, you might say."

"Help!" cried Monkey faintly when he saw the hungry look in Tiger's eyes. "Help!"

Anansi, who had leapt onto a tree, looked down on the two animals below. He thought quickly. "Hey Tiger," he shouted, "I'm glad you're saved but that's Monkey's tail you've got. What are you going to do to him?"

Tiger tried to speak, but of course his mouth was full of tail.

"Pardon?" shouted Anansi. "Sorry, I didn't hear you. Can you speak up?"

"Eat him!" roared the Tiger impatiently, opening his mouth.

But of course the second he let go of the tail, Monkey shot up the nearest tree to safety, well out of Tiger's reach.

"Well I think that's pretty fair," thought Anansi, looking down as the two animals went on their way.

Notes

Follow up themes: help; gratitude; danger.

Anansi, the spider man of West African tradition, has become a folk hero whose stories now entertain world wide audiences.

Concluding prayer:
Let us think this morning about fairness. We all like to be treated fairly and we pray that we can be given strength to avoid being selfish or greedy.
Amen.

13
Winning noisily?

To be modest about our successes is very desirable – as this old tale proves!

Owen Smith's farm was different from most because it had two cockerels in it. Sometimes they took turns to crow on a morning, at other times they both crowed together, and sometimes neither crowed. They were constantly arguing about who was the best at crowing and who therefore should be the master and make all the decisions.

"We must have a contest to find out who is best," exclaimed Cock Number 1.

"I'm ready any time you are," replied Cock Number 2.

"Right," went on the first cock, "tomorrow morning we'll see who can crow loudest for the longest time. Then we'll know who is the master."

The next morning, as dawn crept over the damp and misty fields, the two cocks fluttered to a farmyard fence. Then as the first shafts of daylight broke through they began their crowing. For what seemed like hours both crowed long and loud and then … ever so slowly … Cock Number 2's voice got weaker and weaker. Realising he was going to lose he flapped quietly away into the darkness of a barn.

Cock Number 1 paused in his crowing. "I'm the winner, I'm the winner!" he called out triumphantly. "I'm the best and now I'm master – and what's more I'm going to let everybody know about it!"

So saying he flew to the highest point of the barns and, closing his eyes, he set about crowing as if all the world wanted to hear him.

Indeed one did. High above, an eagle in search of breakfast, heard and then spotted the cock. Swooping down in a flashing dive he silenced the cock in a flurry of wings and swept off with him. Now there was only one cock on the farm – and no arguments about who was the master.

(Adapted from an Aesop's fable)

Notes

Follow up themes: modesty; the way to treat 'winning' and 'losing'.

A thought-provoking Biblical reference in connection with this story is:
"Each man should examine his own conduct for himself; that he can measure his achievement by comparing himself with himself and not with anyone else." *Galatians 6:4.*

Concluding prayer:
Let us think this morning about winning, losing, triumphs and disappointment. Let us pray that we can always try to behave to others as we would like them to behave to us. Amen.

14
A fairy tale

This simple folk tale reminds us of a basic truth – one good turn deserves another.

It was long ago when fields were ploughed by men and horses. Jim was following the plough which was pulled by Daisy and Beth.

"Come on my beauties," called out the old ploughman. "There'll be a good feed for you when we've finished this lot."

As if they understood what he said, the two horses seemed to put an extra zip in their stride as they turned to go up the long field again. Above and behind them the waiting gulls circled noisily and the heat shimmered over the soil.

"On our way again," encouraged Jim.

Five minutes later they were at the other end of the field where a few trees provided a shady turning point.

"Aah," thought Jim to himself, "that churning noise I can hear must be the little folk making their butter."

Like all humans Jim knew it didn't pay to be too curious where the little folk were concerned and he was just wheeling Daisy and Beth round when he heard a voice cry out.

"It's broken, it's broken, my churn staff is broken. What shall I do?"

Before he could help himself the good natured ploughman called out, "Put it out and I'll mend it for you."

Sure enough when he'd done another length of the field and come back, there lying on the grass was the broken staff. Knowing that he would be watched, Jim picked up the staff and turned for another trip up the field.

"Now what can we do here?" he said to himself, when they reached the other end of the field where the bag in which he kept his food, drink and tools lay in the ditch. Quickly he took out a hammer and some of his tiniest nails and mended the staff.

Ten minutes later it was mended and delivered back to the spot where it had lain. Jim went on with his work and soon forgot all about the broken staff.

The afternoon slipped steadily away and Jim turned the horses for their last journey of the day up the field.

"Right my beauties, another day nearly done."

As the tired horses and man came once more to the spot where the broken staff had lain Jim noticed something in the grass. Leaving the handles of the plough he went to investigate. There, in exactly the same spot as they had put the repaired staff, lay something for him. A parcel of freshly made butter and freshly baked bread.

(Adapted from an old Northern folk tale of the North Tyne)

Notes

Follow up themes: kindness; the dignity of work; environmental issues.

A useful prayer which is appropriate here, can be taken from Proverbs 12:14:
One man wins success by his words; another gets his due reward by the work of his hands.

15
Two men and a horse

Sometimes, when we want more, we end up with less – as this story of two men and a horse illustrates.

It had been a good day at the market. Hans and Josef were now making their way home.

"We won't have a better day than that for a while," said Hans happily. He was riding the horse the two men shared between them. Tied behind his saddle and hanging on either of the horse's flanks was the bag containing the money they had made from selling their carvings at the market.

"You're right there," agreed Josef, "but just remember it's soon my turn to ride the horse."

He said this with feeling as he trudged along the wide woodland path. He was thinking ahead to the long climb up to the Alpine village where they lived.

"All right, all right, there's no need to go on about it," replied Hans sourly.

Although they had done well at the market both men were very tired and neither looked forward to when it was their turn to walk rather than ride. Slowly the two emerged from the wood and began the climb upwards.

"Come on," snapped Josef suddenly. "Down you get! My turn now."

"Rubbish," snarled Hans in reply, "we agreed to change when we got to the outcrop of rocks."

"We did no such thing."

"Yes we did."

"Nonsense – now get off that horse before I pull you off!"

For a few more seconds the two men yelled at each other, then Hans grabbed Josef's leg and pulled him from the horse. Furiously Josef tried to push Hans away, and fell off the horse. Breathless and angry they stood standing at each other, fists clenched and eyes blazing angrily.

Meanwhile, startled by the commotion, the horse took flight. Flattening its ears against its head it began to gallop away up the mountain path. Further and further away it went, and then rounding a turn, the saddlebag with all the money in it slipped off and plunged away down the far side of the mountain.

The anger which Hans and Josef had felt fled as suddenly as it had come. Now neither of them had a horse – or any money.

Notes

Follow up themes: sharing; keeping our tempers; concern for others.

Rather than a prayer to end this service, an old African proverb might be more appropriate:

"Hatred is like rain in the desert. It is of no use to anybody."

16
The end of the fight

Arguing often makes us unaware of other dangers which may be threatening – as this old tale illustrates.

"It's time he realised who is the most important person round here," said the mouse, to nobody in particular.

He was talking about the frog. These two creatures had been arguing for weeks, and their arguments often led to fights. The mouse would hide in the long grass and pounce on the frog, and when the frog caught the mouse in the open he would jump on him with all his strength.

"Yes, yes," went on the mouse to himself. "A challenge to a proper fight to settle it all – that's the answer."

Oddly enough the frog was thinking exactly the same thing.

"Now if I beat that mouse in a proper challenge then everybody would know that it was me who was the chief of things round here."

So a great duel was arranged. It was to take place in a large open field, and each creature would be armed with a sword. The one who forced the sword from the other first would be the winner.

Finally the day arrived. The sun shone from a clear blue sky and each of the enemies had his sword – the tip of a bulrush – at the ready. Slowly they advanced towards each other.

"Will you give in now?" said the frog menacingly.

"Ha!" replied the mouse. "You haven't a chance."

High above the field a kite was circling in the sky looking for his dinner. Suddenly he saw the commotion in the field below.

"Easy pickings today," he said to himself with a satisfied smile. Then swooping down he snatched up the mouse and the frog and soared away to his nest to eat.

(Adapted from an Aesop's fable)

Notes

Follow up themes: behaving stupidly, awareness.

A useful quotation here is:
Fools always think they are right; sensible people listen to advice.
(*Proverbs 12:15*)

Concluding prayer:
Let us think this morning about how much we can learn from a simple
story such as we have just heard. Let us learn not to take ourselves too
seriously; not to be impatient with others; but always ready to listen to
good advice. Amen.

17
Greed

It never pays to be greedy – as this tale shows.

Long ago there were two brothers who were left alone when their
father died.
"I'll go to the funeral," said the younger brother sadly. "I'll see you
when I get back."
Now the elder brother, whose name was Simon, was a sly and greedy
man. Whilst his brother was at the funeral he took all the valuable
things his father had left, and hid them. He was waiting for John, the
younger brother, when the funeral was over.
"Hello, John. I'm sorry to have to tell you," he lied, "that father
didn't leave us anything at all."
"Well, never mind," replied John, "at least we've got his house we
can live in."
"I'm afraid not," lied Simon again. "You see, before he died Father
said to me that, because I was married, I could have his house for my
wife and myself."

"Oh," whispered John quietly.

Now, believing his brother, John got on with life as best he could. One day he was working in the fields in the shadow of Mouth Mountain when an amazing thing happened. The mountain, which got its name because it looked as though it had a large mouth in the middle of it, began to shake slightly and ... the mouth opened in a wide yawn.

At first John was terrified ... but then he saw that in the yawning cave in the mountain side were piles of treasure. Rushing inside he quickly filled a sack full of jewels, hurried out and went home.

Well, naturally it wasn't long before Simon heard of John's good fortune.

"How on earth did you come by all this money, brother?" he asked.

"Well, a fantastic thing happened," replied John, "quite fantastic ... listen while I tell you about it."

As Simon listened a strong feeling grew in him – he was going to have some of that treasure – and he was going to be prepared to get a lot.

So, although he had never bothered much before, he began to work in one of the fields in the shadow of Mouth Mountain. And, every day as he laboured there he made sure he had two big carts with oxen tied to them standing in a corner of the field. He was prepared to get plenty of that treasure when the moment came!

The days and weeks went slowly by. Simon was getting rather fed up with this unusual work when, suddenly just before dinner time one day, the mouth in the mountain began to open in a great yawn. There, easy to see, was the pile of treasure.

"Now, now! I must be quick!" Simon gasped breathlessly.

Grabbing a pile of sacks from one of his carts he raced into the cave. Working like a madman he filled one sack with precious jewels, then another, then another, then another ...

"I'll be fifty times as rich as John by the time I'm finished," he chortled.

The Mouth Mountain heard this. "Oh no you won't, you greedy man," he said, and closed his mouth with a bang.

Simon was never seen again.

(Adapted from a Vietnamese folk tale)

Notes

Follow up themes: lies, greed, selfishness.

There is a very appropriate Bible quotation which can be linked to this story:

"The man who loved money can never have enough, and the man who is in love with great wealth enjoys no return from it." *Ecclesiastes 5:10*

Closing prayer:
Dear God, Let us pray this morning that we are content with out fair share of life's blessings. Teach us to beware of greed in all its forms. Amen.

18
What's her name?

A little thought about our own faults is greatly to our advantage.

Have you ever known anybody who always wanted the last word? If you have you'll know how conversations with them go:
   "Will you bring the clothes in please?" "Why should I?"
   or
   "I know a good place to play." "I know a better one."
   or
   ·"My dog's funny." "Mine's funnier."
   Well, long ago in ancient Greece there was a girl who was like this. She drove everybody mad because she just simply had to have the last word every time. She always knew what was faster, bigger, slower, funnier etc. If ever she was asked to do anything there was always a 'why' and she would never be the first to stop if there was an argument.
   Finally a goddess called Hera decided that the girl should be punished because she would not listen to advice.
   "How can we punish her?" asked one of the other gods.

"Yes – what is the best way?" asked another.

"Well, the punishment will have to be severe," said Hera sternly, "and I have decided that this is what it will be. This girl will no longer be able to speak properly – all she will be able to do now will be to repeat the last word anybody says to her."

So the punishment was inflicted on the girl, but when she died sometime later her voice stayed behind forever, crying back that last word from the mountains.

Now, in this story so far, we have not been told the girl's name. Can you guess what it was?

*(The girl's name was, of course, Echo and
the story is an old Greek legend)*

Notes

Follow up themes: ourselves; listening to advice; using words well.

All religions and cultures refer to the enormous potential of the spoken word. In the context of this story the following quotation from the Bible seems relevant:

"The tongue – it is a small member but it can make huge claims. What an immense stack of timber can be set ablaze by the tiniest spark! And the tongue is in effect a fire." *(James 3: 5-6)*

Another useful quotation is:

"Fools always think they are right; sensible people listen to advice." *(Proverbs 12:15.)*

Concluding prayer:

Let us pray this morning that we can be given the common sense to listen to, and act upon, good advice. We pray that we might recognise our own faults as quickly as we see the faults of other people. Amen.

19
Jasper's gold

This story is a reminder of the old saying, 'riches must be used'.

Jasper looked at the old clock ticking away on the mantelpiece. Slowly the hands jerked to 9 o'clock.

"Good," muttered the bearded old man, getting to his feet. "Good, good."

Pausing by the door to trim the wick of his lantern, he then stepped out into the darkness and made his way along the garden path. When he reached the shed at the end of the garden he took a bunch of keys from the pocket of his ragged trousers and unlocked the three locks on the door. Then, crouching on the floor and releasing another lock, he eased up a trapdoor. Reaching inside he brought up a bag and tipped its cascade of gold coins onto the floor.

"Good, good," he muttered as he carefully and lovingly counted the coins. An hour later with everything locked again he made his way back to his ramshackle house where his wife was preparing a supper of the poorest food it was possible to buy.

Every morning and every night Jasper followed the same routine of looking at his gold, feeling and counting it, and then burying it again. So busy was he at this that one morning he failed to see a shadowy figure in the bushes, a shadowy figure which watched him with hungry, greedy eyes.

That night as the pointers on the mantelpiece clock reached 9 again, Jasper prepared for his nightime money count. He had almost reached the shed door when ... he saw that it was ajar, with all locks broken.

"No, no," he gasped, "it can't be ... it can't be."

Crashing into the shed he dragged up the now lockless trapdoor and reached into the hole beneath ... there was nothing there!

"Oh no," wailed the old man, "oh no! My gold, my gold, somebody's taken my gold!"

Hearing the commotion Mary, Jasper's wife, left the house to see what was the matter. For a minute or two she stood in the shed doorway. When she finally spoke her voice was very harsh.

"Well, what are you making such a fuss for," she said, "you might as well keep a bag of stones in there in place of your gold – it was never any use to us when you had it."

Notes

Follow up themes: wealth; what 'being a miser' means in the fullest sense.

A useful Biblical quotation here is:
The man who loves money can never have enough, and the man who is in love with great wealth enjoys no return from it. (*Ecclesiastes 5:10*)

Concluding prayer:
Dear God, help us to realise the importance of sharing our gifts, whatever they may be. Amen.

20
"I want more"

Greed and its consequences are the key features of this story from old Arabia.

Abdalla sat beneath the cool of the tree and looked out at the sun sinking over the desert sand. The journey had been a long one and he and his eighty camels were tired. Of course any man who owned eighty camels was very rich, and Abdalla was looking forward to returning to his splendid house.

"And you, my friend, have you come far?"

Abdalla spoke these words to another traveller who was also resting under the tree. Haroun, the other traveller, had no camels and was travelling on foot.

"From Baghdad," he replied.

Now Baghdad was Abdalla's home and the two men got into a long conversation. Soon they were talking about money.

"Ha, not far from here I know where there is so much treasure that you could load up your eighty camels and that would move only a tiny part of it," said Haroun.

At once Abdalla was interested. He loved money more than anything else. "Tell me more," he said excitedly.

So a bargain was struck. Haroun would lead Abdalla to this fabulous treasure and in return would receive forty camels. The two men and the camels set off.

Soon they reached a steep mountainside and here Haroun stopped and lit a fire. As thick smoke billowed up from the fire he muttered some sharp words and, when the smoke cleared, there was a passage leading to a storeroom crammed with treasure.

Abdalla could hardly believe his luck as the two men crammed gold and jewels into sacks and loaded them onto camels. They had nearly finished when Haroun picked up a small box and carefully put it into a pocket.

"What's in there?" asked Abdalla curiously.

"Oh – just some ointment," replied the other man.

When the loading was complete Haroun re-lit the fire and when thick smoke blew away this time the passageway into the rocks had disappeared. And so the two men, each with their forty camels set off in their separate directions. But already Abdalla was thinking.

"That Haroun – he had nothing when I met him. Now he has forty of my camels. I must try and get some back."

"Friend," said Abdalla. "I've done you no favours. To own forty camels is to have a multitude of worries. Give me ten back and your life will be much easier."

Haroun stroked his chin for a moment. "You're right," he said finally. "Please take them."

Now Abdalla found this persuasion so easy that he asked Haroun for ten more back … then another ten … then another ten. Finally Haroun just stood there with nothing. But Abdalla was still suspicious.

"Well, I think I've done you a favour," he said loudly, "but tell me, that ointment you picked up, what is so special about it?"

Haroun smiled. "Oh, it is very special. If you rub it on your left eye you'll see all the treasures of the world. Here, try some."

So Abdalla rubbed the ointment over his left eye – and immediately saw enormous treasures piled up, riches beyond belief.

"Fantastic," said Abdalla, "and if I rub it on my right eye?"

Haroun hesitated. "You'll go blind in both eyes."

Now Abdalla was tremendously excited by this stage. He'd just got all his camels, plus the treasure they were carrying back. He'd seen all this other treasure. He didn't believe for one moment that the same ointment would make him go blind. He believed that if he rubbed it on his right eye it would show him the way to get to the treasures he had just seen with his left eye. This Haroun was only trying to trick him, thought the shrewd and clever Abdalla.

He rubbed the ointment on his right eye ... and then opened both eyes ... to blackness. He heard Haroun's voice.

"I did tell you, but your greed wouldn't let you listen, Now, what does a blind man want with eighty camels and their treasure?"

So saying, Haroun rode off, leaving Abdalla to beg blindly on the camel trail.

(Adapted from an Arabian story)

Notes

Follow up themes: contentment; greed; sharing good fortune.

Concluding prayer:

Let us pray this morning that we can be free from greed and selfishness. Let us pray that we can be free from envying the things other people might have. Let us pray that we can know the joy of sharing. Amen.

21
The Semi-final

Why do things go wrong? Not being properly prepared is one of the answers to this question – as this story shows.

"We're in the team!"

"Well, I thought we would be, didn't you?"

"Yes … but I never take anything for granted."

"Oh Vicki – you are such a pessimist."

"Well …"

The two girls stood before the school notice board looking at the names in the football team which had been pinned up at playtime. The match was an important one – a cup semi-final, and it was due to be played the next night.

"There's not much time before the game is there?" said Vicki Bywaters, who was one of the school's best midfield players.

"You worry too much," replied Mel Boli, who was the team's best striker. "We'll beat them – no bother!"

At home that night Vicki got her football boots out of the cupboard and inspected them thoroughly. She checked that all the studs were tight and there were no nails sticking up inside. Then she inspected the laces, and finally she cleaned the boots carefully and thoroughly.

Things were rather different at Mel's home.

"Got a match tomorrow night, Mum, so I'll be home late."

"Righto Mel. I hope you win – by the way your Dad looked at your boots the other day and he said they needed new laces."

"Hmm."

"What's more he called at the shops and got you a pair – so make sure you put them in tonight."

"Hmm."

Mel was watching a pop music show on TV and she thought it was just great. It was tea time as soon as it was finished, and after that her big sister let her play some video games on her computer. The night seemed to rush away, and before she knew it she was in bed and just about to go to sleep when … "Oh no, those laces. I forgot all about them … never mind, I'll do them in the morning."

Now Mel wasn't very good at getting up in the morning, so it was no surprise that the next day began with the usual rush.

"Your books, your football boots – have you got them?" called Mum just as she was going to school.

"Oh no … I forgot, Mum – thanks."

"And those laces … did you put them in?"

"Well … er … got to rush, Mum. Thanks – bye."

Hurrying to school Mel thought again about the laces.

"Oh, they'll be all right," she consoled herself. "There'll be no problem."

A few hours later an excited crowd round the pitch cheered and clapped as the cup tie swung first one way and then the other. The teams were evenly matched and neither side could score. Eventually there was only ten minutes left … when it happened.

Vicki burst out of Holly Park's defence and galloped up the field with the ball at her feet. Swerving round the full back she sent a low centre scudding into the goal mouth.

Meanwhile Mel had raced up field in anticipation of such a pass and as the ball swept towards her she took one last long stride ready to crash it into the net. … It was at that moment that her right boot suddenly loosened as the lace snapped and, caught by surprise, she missed the ball completely.

The Merrivale supporters gasped with relief, and then their gasps changed to cheers as the ball was swept from the defence up into attack – and finally into the Holly Park net for the winning goal.

As the teams trudged off, one of the players, head down, trailed behind the rest.

"If only," thought Mel, "if only, if only I'd …"

Notes

Follow up themes: be prepared.

An obvious link with this story is the Biblical one of the girls at the wedding feast. Five of the girls had spare oil for their lamps so that they would be sure they stayed alight until the bridegroom arrived. The other five 'didn't bother' and when their lamps went out they couldn't borrow any oil.

Concluding prayer:
Let us think this morning about how much we can learn from stories of other people. They can help us to see our own mistakes and – more importantly – teach us how to put them right.
Let us pray that we are never caught unprepared.

22
A fisherman's tale

This story is a reminder that if we get something we want by cheating and deception we are always likely to lose it.

There is a very old legend about a fisherman who sailed the rough waters of northern seas. His name was Olaf, and this is what happened to him.

The moon was high in the sky and the wind blew a froth of white from the waves which crashed against the shore. Suddenly ...

"It can't be ... but ..." gasped Olaf to himself. There, in the moonlight before him, a group of young seals had crawled out of the sea. As each one did so the seal skin fell away from it and a beautiful girl appeared. Soon ten girls were dancing on the beach, while the pile of seal skins lay on the sand where they had been left.

"I'd never have never believed it," thought Olaf. "But it's true – once a year seals do come out of the sea and dance as girls on the shore ... and to prove it I'm going to get one of those seal skins."

Sliding silently over the rocks in the moonlight Olaf reached the pile of seal skins, slid one off the top and put it inside his thick jacket. Then, still unseen, he crept back to his cottage.

Hours later, when the red light of dawn lit the northern sky, there was a timid knock on Olaf's door. Surprised at who could be calling so early, the young fisherman opened the door ... and got the shock of this life! Standing there was a beautiful young woman.

"Sir, sir," she said in a very distressed voice, "could you please help me? I am one of the sea folk, and last night while I was dancing on the beach someone stole my seal skin. Without it I can never return to my home in the sea ... oh sir, have you seen a skin anywhere?"

For a minute Olaf couldn't find his voice and then, almost unable to help himself, he did something terribly wrong.

"No, no," he said quickly, "I've seen no seal skin ... no idea what might have happened to it. But come in anyway."

Well, you might guess what happened next. Olaf was young and lonely and the poor girl couldn't return home without her seal skin so, when Olaf asked her to marry him she said yes.

Years past by and Olaf was happy with his beautiful wife who was kind and loving. But when he was out in his boat she wept many bitter tears for hours at the grey, tossing sea.

Olaf had by now forgotten about the seal skin for it was safely hidden in the roof of his cottage where no-one would ever find it. Then, one winter's day when Olaf was out in his fishing boat a terrible storm blew up. Savage waves crashed into his little boat and it was all he could do to stay on board as it was flung madly about in the raging sea.

The wind tore ashore too and Olaf's wife shivered as the cottage groaned and creaked in the tempest. Suddenly a part of the roof was loosened and blew away and something fluttered down from an exposed rafter and landed on the floor. The young woman looked at it. Tears filled her eyes. How could Olaf have deceived her like this? He had been a kind husband but ... slowly she reached down.

Hours later a battered and bruised Olaf reached home. At once he saw the hole in the roof. There was no answer to all his shouts. Scrambling up a ladder he saw the empty space on the rafter where the seal skin had been. Now he knew why there was no wife to greet him. He put his head in his hands and wept.

(Adapted from an old Scandinavian legend)

Notes

Follow up themes: honesty, building on firm foundations, deceit.

There is an appropriate piece of Buddhist advice which could be linked to this story:

"If a man speaks or acts
With an evil thought,
Pain follows him."

Concluding prayer:

Let us pray this morning that we might have the strength to deal with disappointments in our lives and to realise that we cannot have everything we want. We pray that we are never tempted to cheat and deceive people. Amen.

23
Invitation to a party

Making excuses is something we all do from time to time. This story suggests that this is not always a good idea!

Jupiter was planning a fantastic party.

"This is going to be the biggest party ever," he said. "I want everybody to have a really good time and I want every living creature in the world to come."

So the invitations were sent out. All over the world there was great excitement.

"Have you had an invitation to Jupiter's party?"

"Yes – isn't it marvellous!"

"We're all going to his splendid palace."

"Isn't it kind of him."

However, there was one exception in all this pleasure.

"What do I want to go to a party for," moaned the tortoise. "It's nice and comfortable in my house in this ditch. In fact I just don't want to leave my house."

The day of the party arrived. Jupiter's palace was decked out with magnificent lights, and dozens of tables groaned under the weight of all the splendid food. All the creatures arrived on time, which was of course simply good manners, and Jupiter smiled with pleasure as he watched them enjoying themselves. Then ... a frown crossed his face.

"The tortoise," he muttered to himself. "He's not here, and he didn't send me an apology to say he wasn't coming. I wonder ..."

Just then he saw the tortoise come grumpily through the front gate.

"Ah, better late than never," said Jupiter cheerfully. "I'm glad you could come, tortoise. Please – help yourself to whatever you like."

"Hmm," muttered the tortoise rudely, "I didn't really want to come, you know. I was quite content in my little house."

Jupiter was astonished that this creature could be so rude and ungrateful. He spoke again, and this time in a very different voice!

"Is that so?" he said. "Well, if that's how you feel, I command you from this day onwards always to carry your house on your back wherever you go."

And that's how the tortoise has to carry his shell round with him wherever he goes.

(Adapted from Aesop)

Notes

Follow up themes: excuses, gratitude/ingratitude/considering the feelings of others.

Concluding prayer:

Let us think this morning about making excuses, hurting people's feelings, and using words carelessly and hurtfully. Teach us Lord to be unselfish and to consider the feelings of others. Teach us to be grateful and gracious. Amen.

A useful quotation – which might also be used as a prayer is:

"Just a single word that brings peace is better than a thousand useless words." *(From the Dhammapada)*

II

True stories

24
Quick thinking

Courage and quick thinking from children is always impressive – as this motorway story illustrates.

"I'm really looking forward to this training session," said 12 year old Ben Davidson to his friend.

The two boys were on their way to football training at West Bromich Albion and were being driven there by Ben's father in the family Metro. Going at a steady 70mph, Ben watched the traffic flash past on the other side of the motorway.

"Soon be there now," said Ben's father Peter, as he pulled out to overtake a lorry. "I expect that …"

Suddenly and terrifyingly Peter stopped speaking in mid-sentence and with a muffled cry collapsed unconscious at the steering wheel. Immediately the car began to go off the road and onto the central reservation of the motorway. With a cry of panic Ben reached past his unconscious father and grabbed the steering wheel.

The car was going so fast that he couldn't control it properly and it swung violently back into the fast lane and then began to zig zag across all three lanes. Dodging other traffic, Ben fought to control the speeding car and direct it towards the hard shoulder of the road. Eventually he reached it and as the car sped along it he took a firm hold of the hand brake, and with a shout of "Hold tight," he pulled it as hard as he could. With a squeal of tyres the speeding vehicle screeched and slithered to a halt.

Without a second's hesitation Ben leapt out. "Got to get help for Dad," he called aloud as he began to flag down the oncoming traffic.

Seeing what had happened several other cars stopped and soon Peter Davidson was being rushed to hospital. Thanks to Ben's courage and quick thinking a terrible motorway crash had been averted and his father's life had been saved.

"I didn't have much time to think about it," said the modest boy afterwards.

Notes

Follow up themes: courage, quick thinking.

The Davidsons were from Redditch, Hereford and Worcestershire.

A relevant Biblical passage is:
Prepare yourself for testing. Set a straight course, be resolute. Do not lose your head in time of disaster. *Ecclesiasticus 2:1-2*

Concluding prayer:
Let us pray this morning for courage in unexpected situations. Let us pray that at such times we would not be hesitant and afraid but would have the speed and resourcefulness to take positive action. Amen.

25
One more try

So often rescue attempts are successful because the searchers are prepared to have one more try.

Once again a climber was lost in the Scottish Highlands and the emergency services had been alerted …

The helicopters buzzed like angry bees over the Scottish mountain tops.

"Not much fuel left, skipper," said Steve Wood the observer, checking the machine's fuel gauge.

"You're right, but I just have a feeling …"

Flight Lieutenant Paul Farrant, the pilot and captain of the helicopter, eased the controls to starboard as he scanned the barren landscape beneath him.

"That crevasse down there," he muttered, "there's something that looks like a red fern growing from the side deep down in it."

"OK Skip," replied Steve Wood, "I'll watch on the next pass."

Again the helicopter thundered over the deep crevasse, and as it did so Paul Farrant let out a triumphant shout.

"It's not a fern – it's a red shirt!"

"You're right skipper, I'll set up winching operations."

A few minutes later the machine was hovering over the deep slash in the top of the mountain, and the winchman was being lowered. This was a tense moment for the crew: a gust of wind or a slight miscalculation on the pilot's part could mean disaster for them all.

"He's down!" called Steve Wood as he watched the winchman come to rest on a ledge 80 feet down in the crevasse. "And he's found the climber."

Down below, deep into the crevasse and on a ledge which was only five feet wide, the winchman worked desperately to get the lost and injured climber strapped onto a stretcher. When he had finished this difficult and dangerous task he waved a hand and the lifting operation began. Soon helicopter and all on board were speeding to the hospital which had been alerted by radio.

"The rescue team did an absolutely marvellous job!"

So said Judith David, the injured man's sister-in-law sometime later.

"Robert, my brother-in-law had been missing for four days and four nights when they found him. For most of this time he was lying injured on a five foot ledge, having fallen 80 feet. If he'd slipped again he would have gone down another 75 feet to certain death. Those rescue boys were just great!"

Notes

Follow up themes: try, try, try again; being responsible; those who help us.

Robert Sparkes, aged 57, was climbing north east of Glen Etive in Argyllshire when the accident occurred. He suffered a broken arm, and back and leg injuries.

Concluding prayer:

Let us give thanks for all those people who help us in so many different ways. Let us also pray that we have the wisdom to behave sensibly as much as we can so that the lives of others are not endangered in trying to save ours. Amen.

26
Thinking of others

When your own life has been increasingly difficult it is a wonderful thing to be able to think of others.

"Faster, faster!"

The two men in the stolen car thought of only one thing – escape. The passenger urged the driver to even greater speed as they accelerated away from the street where they had stolen the car.

"Once we're round this corner we'll be safe ... look out!"

The teenage girl was crossing the road right in front of the speeding car. It couldn't possibly miss her and there was a terrifying thud as the near side door hurled her down the steps and into the basement of a nearby hotel.

It was nearly two weeks later when Jennifer recovered consciousness and found herself in a hospital bed. Serious faces were bending over her.

"Now, don't worry Jennifer, you will be able to walk again. But it will take a long time – perhaps two years."

As Jennifer listened to these words she felt a fierce determination flood through her.

"I'm certainly going to walk again – and much sooner than they think," she thought silently to herself.

So the healing process began and Jennifer astonished everybody with her courage and determination. Soon she was back at school, and attending daily physiotherapy sessions at hospital.

"What marvellous progress she's making," said the doctors to each other but Jennifer continued to surprise them. As soon as she could walk again without any help she made an announcement to everybody she knew.

"I don't think sufficient people realise what a wonderful job our hospitals do – look how they've helped me for instance. I'm going to start fund raising for Glan Clwyd Hospital."

So, as well as putting her own life back together, this brave girl started a money raising appeal and soon she was responsible for collecting £11,300 to buy life saving equipment for her local hospital.

"What a girl," said her doctor, "and what she's done to help others too!"

Notes

Follow up themes: misfortune, helping others, health, hospitals.

Jennifer Chrisensen was given only a 10% chance of survival after her accident. The money she raised was for the Glan Clwyd Hospital in Bodelwyddan, North Wales where she was taken after the accident, and the Arrowe Park Hospital, Birkenhead where she received physiotherapy.

On March 10th 1986 Jennifer was given the Arrow-Ross McWhirter Young Citizen's Award.

This morning's prayer:

Dear God, Please help those people who behave recklessly to have more control and care for others; please help those people who are hurt or injured to have the will, courage and determination to get well; please help doctors and nurses in their work; please help all of us to be more aware of the needs of other people. Amen.

27
Heroes

Heroes are people we admire for their famous deeds – but sometimes their less famous deeds make us admire them more.

"What's he doing?"
"He's going for a swim, isn't he?"
"Yes – but why dive off the end of the pier?"
The people who were talking were on the beach at Dover. It was August 24th, 1875 and they had just seen a burly man in brilliant red swimming trunks dive off the end of the pier. They were quite right, he was going for a swim – twenty one miles of one to be exact, all the way to France!
The swimmer was twenty seven year old Matthew Webb and he

started his swim knowing that ahead of him lay possible storms, sea sickness, intense cold, powerful and variable tides and plenty of stinging jellyfish.

Settling down, the well built English sea captain pulled ahead patiently with his breast stroke dropping into a rhythm of twenty two strokes a minute. Alongside him a lugger kept pace, ready to give him beef tea, brandy, cod-liver oil and coffee to keep his strength up.

By 11pm on the night of 24th August all seemed to be going well. Webb had covered twelve and a half miles and had only eight miles to go. Less good however was the fact that he was cold, desperately tired and had been stung by eight jellyfish. Now the real struggle started.

The tide turned against him and his even more wearied strokes seemed only to keep him swimming on the spot.

"He's not making any progress at all," said one of the ship's crew.

"You're right, I expect the skipper'll ask us to haul him aboard any second."

But Matthew Webb wouldn't come aboard and would not give up. Now, swept eastwards by the tide, he was having to come far more than the twenty one miles of the direct route from Dover to Cap Gris Nez, but he still persisted even if agonisingly slowly.

"You've got to admire his courage," said the skipper of the lugger.

"I think he'd rather sink than give up," replied the mate.

Hour after hour the struggle went on until finally the brave swimmer felt his feet touch the ground. Twenty one hours and forty five minutes after he had dived off Dover Pier, Matthew Webb staggered ashore in France. Bruised by the slapping of the waves, stung by jellyfish and utterly exhausted, he had done what no man had ever done before – swum the English Channel.

So Matthew Webb became a hero, as famous in France as he was in England. Everywhere people admired his courage, determination and refusal to give in when faced with difficulties.

But there was more to Matthew Webb than that, and as people sought to find out more about him even more heroic deeds came to light.

When he had been only ten years old and living in Shropshire he had dived into the River Severn to rescue his brother from drowning. Then, as a young man he had jumped off a Mersey Ferry to rescue a passenger who had fallen overboard. In 1874 he had been awarded the Royal Humane Society's Stanlope gold medal for swimming for nearly half an hour in a raging Atlantic gale when trying to rescue a seaman who had been blown off his ship by the ferocious wind.

Matthew Webb was not only brave and determined, but he was always ready to risk his own life in using his strength and skill to save others.

Notes

Follow up themes: courage; determination; life saving skills.

At the time of his achievement Webb's cross Channel feat was regarded as possibly the greatest feat of endurance in the world of sport. It was achieved without any of the modern additions of goggles, increased knowledge of tides or weather forecasts.

Sadly Webb's life ended tragically when, despite all advice, he tried to swim the rapids below Niagara Falls. He drowned in the attempt on July 24th, 1883.

A useful address for sea rescue follow up work is: Royal National Mission to Deep Sea Fishermen, 43 Nottingham Place, London WIM 4BX.

The following is a useful Bible reference in connection with this story:

Let us now sing the praises of ... the heroes of our nation's history ... Their lives endure for all time and their fame will never be blotted out ... and God's people will sing their praises. *Ecclesiasticus 44:1, 13-15*

The service could end with the following prayer:

Let us give thanks this morning for those people who have exceptional strength, skill and courage and who are, so often an inspiration to us all. Amen.

28
The prayer

Finding a burglar in your room would be very frightening. This story tells of how one woman dealt with that situation.

"Right – I'm in," muttered Tom to himself through clenched teeth. "Now to find a room with something worth stealing in it."

Tom was desperate. No job, no money, no home, he was forced to steal to stay alive. Now, inside a hotel, he was creeping stealthily up the stairs ready to break into the first room he could find.

Seconds later he was in a neat and tidy single room. From the things which were in the room he could tell that the person staying here was a woman.

"Good, good," he thought to himself, "that means jewellery, and maybe some expensive stuff at that."

Methodically he began his search. Dressing tables drawers, stacked cases, clothes in the wardrobe were all inspected minutely. So far he had discovered nothing of value, and Tom was getting frustrated.

Just at that moment he heard approaching footsteps. They stopped outside the door and he heard the rattling of a key. What was he to do?

"The bed!" he thought desperately, and in one frantic movement he threw himself onto the floor and squeezed agonisingly into the narrow space under the bed.

He heard the door open, and shut. Then he saw a pair of lady's feet moving about the bedroom. Various things were put down and then the feet suddenly stopped. For a moment or two they remained where they were.

"Please ... please go out again," thought Tom in panic.

Then the feet moved towards the bed – and stopped about a foot from it. There was the sound of clothes rustling and two knees came onto the floor about two inches from Tom's face. The bed gave a creak as someone rested on it.

To Tom's amazement the lady started to speak, but not, as he thought at first, to him. It took him a second or two to realise that she was kneeling beside the bed praying. As he listened to the prayers he felt strange feelings coming over him, particularly as the words went on

"... and now, Lord, hear my prayers about the person who is hiding under this bed. He must be desperately unhappy to be there, and awful circumstances must have driven him to break into this room. Please Lord, let him know that he can be helped and ..."

Almost without realising what he was doing, Tom crawled slowly out from under the bed, got onto his knees and closed his eyes. He stayed there silently until the lady had finished praying. Then opening his eyes he looked into one of the kindest faces he had ever seen.

"Now," said the lady, "let's sit down and see how I can help."

Notes

Follow up themes: forgiveness; faith; prayer.

This story is based on the occasion when Elizabeth Fry, the great eighteenth century prison reformer, was staying in a hotel in Bristol, and happened to notice that there was a burglar hiding under her bed.

Elizabeth Fry (1780–1845) was also a notable preacher and belonged to the Society of Friends. This story could be linked to the one about the Earl of Shaftsbury, which is also in this section.

A useful Biblical quotation here might be:

Let all bitterness and wrath and anger ... be put away from you. *Ephesians 4 v 31*

Prayer:

Dear God, Help us to learn how to forgive people and teach us to be more tolerant when we are irritated or annoyed or worried. Amen.

29
Accident!

Would you be prepared to risk your life to save a dog?

The dry and dusty road stretched long and straight under the hot African sun. Potholes and loose stones made travelling over it uncomfortable and dangerous – as the men in the lorry knew very well.

"I'll be glad to get there, Pete," muttered the driver, gripping the steering wheel with clenched fists.

"You're right," replied Peter Randall, " but it must be even more hot and uncomfortable for those lads and Rex in the back."

The men in the lorry were all soldiers and Rex, the dog, was their mascot.

"Nearly there anyhow …" went on the driver.

"Ye … Look out!"

Pete's cry was too late. The lorry hit a huge pothole and the steering wheel was wrenched out of the driver's desperate hands. For what seemed an age the truck skidded sideways along the road and then, with a tremendous roar, the petrol tank exploded.

Flames leapt round the overturned lorry and Peter Randall, ignoring the pain of his own injuries, kicked open the passenger door and dragged the unconscious driver out to safety.

"Must check the others," was his next thought.

Limping round to the rear of the lorry he found that all of the other soldiers had crawled out of the now blazing wreck, but …

"Where's Rex?" he demanded.

"He's still in there, Corporal, he's …"

Pushing the man aside Peter scrambled through the flames into the back of the lorry. Once inside he released the leash which had been holding Rex fast, and led the terrified dog to safety. Back on the road Rex nuzzled his master's hand as the corporal looked round.

"Right," exclaimed Peter, and held the leash out to one of the least injured soldiers. "You take care of Rex while I go and get help."

Then, despite the pain of his wounds, Corporal Peter Randall limped down the road for nearly a quarter of a mile. There he found a camp and got help.

The story had a happy ending. Rex recovered completely from his injuries and Corporal Randall received the George Medal for his bravery. He also received another special medal from the RSPCA for saving Rex's life.

Notes

Follow up themes: caring for animals.

This incident took place in 1955 and Corporal Randall was the first soldier from the Royal Army Veterinary Corps' history to win the George Medal.

Follow up themes: courage; animals; concern for others.

A useful comment for further discussion is:
It is important to give help to friend before enemy, young before old, man before animal.

Some interesting opinions often arise from a consideration of this statement.

Closing prayer:
Let us pray this morning for all animals, and those who look after them. May we be thankful for the pleasure given to us by all pets. Amen.

30
Robbed!

Having a good reputation sometimes brings unexpected rewards, as even a burglar found out in this story.

"It's no good looking any more – they're gone and that's the end of it."
   The man spoke to himself. Coming home late at night he had found

all the signs that his house had been burgled. Worst of all though, he discovered that a gold watch and chain were missing.

"Oh I know they're valuable," he muttered to himself, " but it's the fact that they were a present from Jean which upsets me so much."

Jean had been the man's nurse long ago in childhood and when he had become a young man she had scrimped and saved to buy him this special present – and now it was gone, lost forever.

With a sigh the man sat down on the edge of a hard chair. Many people would have been sad to see him distressed because he was the Earl of Shaftesbury, famous throughout the country for helping other people. For years he had worked to stop children being used as slaves in coal mines, and as chimney sweeps. He had helped to set up better schools and spent long weekends and evenings touring the back streets of London giving help wherever he could to the poorest of people. There was nobody who didn't like and admire the Earl of Shaftesbury.

The next morning he mentioned his loss to a few people and immediately the news began to spread round London.

"Have you heard?"

"No – what?"

"Earl of Shaftesbury's been robbed."

"Never!"

"No – it's right. Hard to believe though isn't it?"

"Hard to believe, why ... it's ... it's criminal that's what it is!"

A week passed and one evening the Earl of Shaftesbury was just about to sit down to his evening meal when there was a tremendous crash against his front door.

"What the ..."

Leaving his food he quickly rushed to the door and opened it. There, lying on the step was a sack, and what's more the sack was moving!

Bending down the Earl wrenched the knots at the sack's neck free and saw inside a dirty, struggling boy who had both his hands tied behind his back. Round his neck was a watch and chain which the Earl recognised immediately, and stuffed into the boy's scruffy jacket was a note.

"Here's your thief. Do with him as you please," said the note.

Two hours later man and boy sat facing each other. The boy had freely confessed to stealing the watch, but had also told the Earl that he had no parents, no home and no money, and the only way he could stay alive was by stealing.

Long into the night the two talked. The boy promised he would never steal again and the man promised he would help the boy to find a school and learn a trade. Both promises were kept and the boy grew up to be a respectable, hard working, honest man.

Notes

Follow up themes: helping others; honesty; reputations; hardships.

Some useful material could be obtained from Save the Children Fund, Mary Datchelor House, 17 Grove Lane, Camberwell, London SE5 8RD.

A useful Biblical reference/prayer to end the service could be:
Blessed are those who show mercy;
Mercy shall be shown to them.
Matthew 5:7

(Useful link with 'The prayer' in the True Stories section)

31
The coin

This is an inspiring story of the concern and consideration poor people sometimes have for each other.

"How are we going to get some money to feed our families?" asked Bert anxiously.

"Certainly not by working – there's just nobody can get a job at the moment," said Alf.

"Why don't we entertain people – you know – sing in the streets?" suggested John.

Anything was worth a try. This was England during the great Depression of the 1930s, when millions of people had no work and were desperately poor.

So Bert, Alf and John and more of their friends got together and practised singing. To their surprise they were very good and sang beautifully. Finally, after lots of practice they went to the middle of a long street in the village and sang for nearly an hour. When they had finished Bert started at one end of the street, and John at the other, asking people if they could spare a little money to help feed the singers' families.

Mrs Allen, an old lady who lived by herself, was cooking when John came to her door. Although she was rather flustered and in a bit of a hurry she found time to speak to him.

"That singing was lovely," she said. "All those old songs – you sang them so well. Here, I hope this will help."

Hurriedly she reached into the tin box where she kept her money and gave John a coin. Smiling as she watched him go down the street she was about to put the lid on the tin when she glanced inside and saw that she given him the wrong coin – for an amount she certainly couldn't afford.

"Oh dear," she said to herself. "Well, I'll just have to go without a bit of food this week that's all."

Meanwhile John, Bert, Alf and the others were counting the small coins they had collected. When John scooped the little pile out of his cap he saw the old lady's coin gleaming – and realised at once what must have happened.

Some time later Mrs Allen was washing up when there was a knock at the door.

"Hello again," she said to John, when she opened the door and saw him standing there.

"Hello," said John, "and thanks for helping us out, but I know you couldn't afford to give us this."

So saying he handed back the coin Mrs Allen had given him by mistake.

Notes

Follow up themes: money; concern for others; kindness.

There is an old Ghanaian proverb which seems appropriate to the thoughts provoked by this story:

If you talk to gold it will not answer you.
If you talk to cloth it will not answer you.

What really counts,
Is man.

Concluding prayer:
Let us think this morning about the words of a famous old prayer: "Let us learn to give and not to count the cost, work and not look for rest or think about what is the reward." *(Adapted from St Ignatius)*

32
The story of Iqbal Masih

This is a very sad story – but a very important one. It is about a boy who knew he had to do something to help others.

"All right – we'll sell him," said the man.
"Good, I'll give you a fair price," said the factory owner.
"When do you want him then?"
"Oh now, I'll take him right away."
The two men were talking about the first man's son. His name was Iqbal Masih. He was four years old.
After Iqbal was sold by his father he was taken to a carpet factory. There he was chained to a weaving loom to help make carpets. Now he had to work for the money the owner of the factory had paid to his father.
For six long years Iqbal slaved away, his tiny fingers making the smallest, tightest knots which older fingers couldn't manage. His whole life was simply work, work, work.
When Iqbal was freed from his slavery he knew he must do something to help the millions of other children, all over Pakistan, who from the youngest of ages worked in factories, or farms, made bricks or were the most menial of servants.
"I must tell people what is happening," thought Iqbal, "not only here in Pakistan, but all over the world."
As you can imagine that was not easy but there were groups of other

people who wanted to stop these dreadful things too. When they heard what Iqbal had to say they arranged for him to go to Sweden. There, at an international conference, he told many people about the horrors he had suffered, and how so many other children were still suffering them.

"What a fantastic boy," said one listener.

"I agree," replied another.

"Well, I'm going to see that more people hear about this," went on another man. "Next month in Boston, USA, they are going to present a special award for Youth in Action. I think Iqbal deserves to win it."

"We agree," said practically everybody else there.

So in December 1994 Iqbal Masih, the small, now twelve year old slave labourer from a Pakistan village, flew to America. There he was given the Reebok Youth in Action Award and a prize of £9,670. "I didn't know there was so much money in the world," joked Iqbal. "I'm going to use it making up for all the schooling I've missed. Then I hope to go on to be a lawyer and when I become one I'll be in a better position to help all those desperately miserable children in Pakistan who are still suffering as I did."

"He deserves as much help as he can get," said the many Americans who heard Iqbal. Some of them belonged to a university near Boston and they sent a message to Iqbal.

"As soon as you are ready," they said, "we would like you to come to this university to study to be a lawyer. We'll give you a full scholarship which means you won't have to pay anything."

Well, as you can imagine, Iqbal was thrilled.

"I'm going back home to Pakistan to study," he said, "and then I'll be back to take my scholarship. I can't wait to become a lawyer and do something about these evil men who make children's lives so miserable."

So Iqbal went back to Pakistan. Now remember he was still only twelve, and twelve year old boys have lots of energy and like to enjoy themselves.

"Come on," he said to two of his friends shortly after he had got back. "Let's go for a bike ride."

So the three youngsters set out for a ride in a village near Lahore. As they pedalled along a shot suddenly rang out … and Iqbal Masih fell from his bike … he was dead.

Notes

Follow up themes: courage; causes for concern; childhood; justice.

The dramatic and tragic end to this story leaves possible explanations to the teacher. The *Daily Telegraph* of April 19th, 1995 quoted Mr. Ehsan Ullah Khan of the Bonded Labour Liberation Front as saying … "He was so brave, we know his death was a conspiracy by the carpet mafia."

There are two Bible readings which are particularly appropriate here. Either, or both, could be used as concluding prayers:

Let us never tire of doing good, for if we do not slacken our efforts we shall in due time reap our harvest. Therefore, as opportunity offers, let us work for the good of all. *Galatians 6: 9-10*

There is no greater love than this, that a man should lay down his life for his friends. *John 15:13*

33
Saved!

Team spirit can sometimes work wonders – as this horse rescue story shows.

"I'm going to take my horse down to the water's edge to cool off," shouted Emma to her two friends, Melanie and Iona.

"Good idea," called Melanie. "Let's go."

With a flick of the reins the girls sent their horses cantering towards the edge of the incoming water. They were riding on the beach near Cardross on the Clyde Estuary.

Laughing and joking as their hair blew in the wind the girls neared the water's edge – and then disaster struck. The firm sand changed to thick mud in a matter of yards and within seconds the horses' feet stuck in the mud and the girls, not expecting the sudden stop, fell off.

"Get them out – quickly!" screamed Emma, as the horses began to slowly sink.

She leapt back onto her horse Mucsha and tried to urge it out of the mud. It was no use.

"Look," cried Melanie desperately, "the tide."

Sure enough the tide was coming in rapidly bringing ever deeper water to swirl round the struggling, sinking horses. It was then that the girls heard the shout.

"Hang on, hang on! Help's on the way."

Two men had seen the difficulties the girls and horses were in. One had gone to raise the alarm and the other was coming to help them.

Within a short time more help had arrived. Firemen, lifeboat crews, coast guards and others arrived on the scene. Quickly the firemen used hoses and air bags to support the horses while others urged the animals to try and stand to get themselves out of the mud.

By now however the horses were terrified and exhausted. They wouldn't or couldn't stand, and began to sink deeper and deeper into the mud and onrushing water.

Then John Gorrie, one of the life boatmen shouted, "We'll have to drag them out!"

"Girls – you hold their heads above the water," called a fireman urgently.

So the desperate struggle continued. Now almost up to their waists in water the rescuers either held or pulled the heavy, terrified horses. Inch by inch the creatures were edged out of the cloying death until, finally, men, girls, and animals lay exhausted but safe on firm sand once more.

"We just didn't know how dangerous the beach was," said Iona later.

"But the help we got was absolutely great," said Emma.

Team work saved the day.

Notes

Follow up themes: danger; working together; being prepared.

This incident took place on a Saturday evening in June.

Teachers may find it interesting to know that in Biblical time when the Persians wanted to honour a man he was dressed in splendid clothes and led through the streets astride a horse. *(Esther 6, 9-11).*

A useful prayer might be:
Dear God, Teach us to value the help we get from so many people, not just in moments of crisis, but throughout every day of our lives. Amen.

34
Saving Scrap

St Francis was a man who saved many animals – and there are many people like him in the modern world.

"No, Scrap, no!"

David Commons was out for a walk with his dog when he saw her heading for a hole on the wooded hillside of Crosland Hill, Huddersfield.

"Scrap … keep away from that hole!"

David's shouts were in vain. Without stopping, the curious terrier headed straight for the hole, nosed around the entrance, then disappeared. By the time an anxious Mr Commons reached the hole there was no sign of the animal. Bending down and looking in as far as he could David could see nothing and his shouts brought no response at all from Scrap.

"She must be trapped down there," David thought, "probably gone in deep and can't turn round to get back. I'll have to get a spade and dig down."

Hurrying back home, David collected a spade and told a friend what had happened. Within a short time both men were hard at work digging as fast as they could.

"This is hard work!"

"There are so many stones – they're slowing our progress."

"Never mind – we'll have a rest when it gets dark and start early in the morning."

Desperately as the two men worked, digging and scraping with their bare hands, they made only slow progress. Day followed night and they dug on through much of the next night and day.

"Do you think … ?" wondered David's hard working neighbour.

"No I don't," interrupted David quickly. "I'm sure she's not dead and I'm sure she's trapped down there somewhere. But we're going to need extra help to rescue her."

So after four days of unsuccessful work, a team of helpers gathered beside the now enlarged hole through which Scrap had disappeared.

"OK, let's go!" shouted a digger driver as he engaged the gears of his huge machine which began scooping out great mounds of earth. Deeper and deeper it dug, until there was a huge crater in the hillside.

"I think that should be enough," called out an RSPCA Inspector who was also on the scene. "I'll go down and investigate."

"I'm coming with you," said David Commons determinedly.

So the two men lowered themselves into the huge hole and began digging downwards through a smaller passage.

Deeper and deeper they went until …

"She's here!"

"Where?"

"She's lying in a crevice underneath a giant boulder."

"Is she all right?"

"Well, I can see her tail wagging!"

The rest of the team swung into action. As David and the RSPCA inspector eased the frightened dog from her tiny safety spot she barked with gratitude. Then they passed her back along the line of three more RSPCA inspectors and eight firemen who had all come to help.

Finally men and dog were all back on the surface of the hillside.

"She must have been more than 30 feet down," said one of the firemen.

"You're right there," agreed an RSPCA inspector, "and there must have been hundreds and hundreds of tons of stones, soil and rubble lying on that rock she was underneath."

"It's a miracle she survived," muttered another man.

"Perhaps," said David, "but it's a miracle which couldn't have happened without the help of all you people. I'm very grateful to all of you – and so is Scrap."

As if she knew what was being said there was a sudden, chirpy bark of agreement from the little terrier.

Notes

Follow up themes: determination; team work; animals.

Useful address: RSPCA, Causeway, Horsham, West Sussex RH12 1HG.

For a concluding prayer the following adaptation from Psalm 104 might be used:

Countless things are made by your hand,
And the earth is full of your creatures.
All of them look to you
To give them food at the proper time.
What you give them they gather up;
When you open your hand they eat their fill.
May your glory stand forever
And may you rejoice in your works.

35
Sledge to the rescue

This is the story of quick thinking, a daring rescue, and modesty.

During the Second World War London was bombed many times and people became used to the sound of fire brigade bells ringing and the sight of burning houses, shops and factories.

"Another raid," thought Jimmy as he walked along a London Street. "Just when I'm on leave too!"

The sirens, warning of the oncoming enemy bombers, wailed their mournful cry and people began to run towards the air raid shelter. It was a warm May night and the leaves fluttering gently in the breeze seemed a cheerful contrast to the ruins of the city.

Then the enemy planes were overhead and bombs began to whistle downwards. Before Jimmy could take cover a bomb hit a house nearby and it immediately started to burn.

"Help ... help ...!"

Jimmy heard the desperate cries from the upstairs part of the house. Quickly he took in the situation. A man and woman were trapped upstairs, the bottom part of the house was blazing and if they weren't rescued soon they would certainly die. There were no fire engines or rescue services in sight.

"I'm coming!" yelled Jimmy, and he raced towards the house. The front door was closed but, seeing a fire iron lying on the ground nearby, Jimmy jammed it underneath the hinges and tore the door off its frame.

Keeping the fire iron in his hand, and holding his handkerchief over his face he dashed up the stairs, ignoring the flames as he did. Then, at the top of the stairs, he found the bedroom door tightly shut too.

"I'll be with you in a second!" he called and, ramming the fire iron beneath the hinges, again he tore off the second door.

Inside the bedroom were two old people. Jimmy saw at a glance that they would no be able to run down the stairs quickly enough to avoid being badly burned.

"Don't worry. I've got a great idea," he muttered encouragingly to the terrified couple.

Turning back he laid the bedroom door flat at the top of the stairs. Then quickly going into the bedroom he hustled the man and woman out and told them to sit on the door.

"Right," he shouted. "We're going to use this door as a sledge. When I shout "Go!" I'll push it off and we'll be down those stairs before you can blink!"

By now smoke and crackling flames filled the staircase, but using his right foot to push it off, Jimmy sent the door on its way down the stairs, jumping onto it at the last minute.

Like a great, flat sledge the door swished down the stairs and rocketed straight out through the front door and into the safety of the street.

The man and the woman were astonished, confused – and grateful.

"You've saved our lives young man," cried the woman.

"Are you all right?" asked Jimmy, as he helped them from the life saving door.

"Thanks to you we are," said the man, "you must let us ..."

But he was talking to thin air! The hero, having done his job, had simply vanished.

Notes

Follow up themes: courage; fire; war; peace.

The hero was traced. He was Commander Jimmy Crews and in 1943 he was awarded the George Medal for his bravery. The incident took place on May 21st, 1941.

A useful address is: The London Fire Brigade, 8 Albert Embankment, London SE1 7SD. They have an interesting museum: Brigade Museum, Winchester House, 94a Southwark Bridge Road, London SE1 OEX.

A concluding prayer might be:

Let us think this morning about the daring and courage of men like Jimmy. We pray that we may never be at war again, but accidents still happen. When they do so many people are grateful for the courage, skill and daring of others. Amen.

36
You're never too young

How old have you to be, to be brave, quick thinking, ready to save others? As these true stories show, perhaps we should say 'how young have you to be?'

"Just going to do some work on the car."

Robert's dad called out this message as he went outside to work on his car. Robert followed, stood in the doorway, and watched his dad open the boot of the car.

Mr Marsh started to jack the car up so that he could work underneath it. Robert watched, fascinated, as his dad, with just a few turns of the jack handle, lifted the heavy car high off the ground on one side. Mr. Marsh then lay on the ground and eased himself under the car to see what the problem was. But when he was completely underneath there was a sudden creaking and groaning from the jack, and then with a startling bang, the jack collapsed and the car crashed to the ground.

Robert was horrified. "Dad, Dad," he cried, "are you all right? Are you all right?

There was a groan from under the car. "Yes ... I think so son ... but I'm trapped under here. I'll need some help to get me out."

"But what can I do, Dad?"

"Well ... listen carefully. Go inside and lift up the telephone. Then press the button with '9' on it three times. Somebody will answer you. Say to them that your dad is trapped under a car and tell them our address. Do you think you can do that?"

Robert paused for a minute, trying to remember all his father had told him. All the time he was also trying very hard not to cry.

"I think I can do it, Dad."

Nervously the boy went into the house and did exactly what his father told him to do. The voice on the other end of the telephone was very kind and told him not to worry and that somebody would be there to help very, very soon.

Robert went back outside.

"Are you all right Dad?"

"Yes I'm still OK, Robert. Can you tell me what happened when you used the telephone?"

Robert started to tell his dad, but before he had even finished he heard the 'dah-doh' of a fire engine coming. Everything was going to be all right! Now, this was exciting.

Robert Marsh was four years old.

Our next young hero was older than Robert but he did something that needed a great deal of skill as well as a lot of courage.

His name is Jon and he was with his father when there was an accident. Mr McNestrie cut an artery in his arm. This meant that blood came out of the cut very quickly and it had to be stopped before Mr McNestrie bled to death.

"OK," cried Jon, seeing what had happened. "I know what to do, I've learnt about it in First Aid. I must put a tourniquet on to stop the bleeding."

A proper tourniquet is a bandage which must be pressed extra specially tight on a cut artery to stop the blood flowing out. Jon had no bandages but using handkerchiefs and twisting one to tighten the others he managed to stop the bleeding. Then checking to see that his father was as well as he could be, he hurried off and phoned 999.

Soon an ambulance arrived.

"Well done son," said one of the ambulance men as they helped Mr McNestrie into the ambulance. "You made a wonderful job of his tourniquet – a doctor couldn't have done it better – and your dad might have died if you hadn't got it on when you did."

Jon McNestrie was twelve years old.

Notes

Follow up themes: 999; people who help us; be prepared.

An annual source for inspiring stories like this is the Children of Courage Award Service in Westminster Abbey which takes place every December. Children are always very impressed when they hear of some of the courageous exploits of their peers.

A useful prayer to end this service might be:

Let us pray this morning that we may be brave and cool thinking if we are ever suddenly and unexpectedly called upon to help others as Robert and Jon were. Let us pray that we can learn as much as possible to be prepared if we are ever needed in emergencies. Amen.

37
Skydiver

There are many different kinds of courage. This story is about the type where instant decisions and actions must be taken.

The sixteen men were taking part in an international skydiving event over France. The giant Hercules aircraft droned through the sky 15,000 feet above the ground while the parachutists inside prepared to make their jumps.

"OK, Maurice, your turn."

Andy Peckett gave the thumbs up to Italian Maurizio Brambilla as the latter got ready to jump.

"Now!"

Brambilla lunged out of the aircraft and began to plunge earthwards. What nobody else on the plane had realised however, was the Italian had hit his head on a rear exit ramp on the way out and had knocked himself unconscious.

Meanwhile Andy watched his falling colleague. At first he thought nothing was wrong and then, after about ten seconds, he realised that Maurizio was not falling properly and was not reaching for his parachute's rip cord.

"Something's wrong!" yelled Andy, and at the same time he flung himself head first out of the aircraft.

"I've got to catch Maurizio before he is too low to open his 'chute," he thought to himself as he whistled through the air.

Andy was an experienced jumper and he knew that the fastest way to fall was to keep the head pointing downwards. So at 200 miles per hour Andy Peckett fell through one and a half miles of sky in seconds.

Finally, 5,000 feet above the ground, Andy reached the unconscious Italian. He could see blood on Brambilla's face and knew that his friend could not help himself. Clinging onto Maurizio's body Andy began feeling desperately for the ripcord of his parachute.

"If only I could turn him over to get to this ripcord," he thought desperately, as the two men rocketed towards the rapidly approaching earth.

4,000 feet ... 3,500 feet ... 3,000 feet ... 2,500 feet.

"Got it," cried Andy in relief as his fingers closed on Maurizio's rip cord. He pulled it firmly and as the pair plunged beneath 2,000 feet there was a crack as Brambilla's parachute opened and billowed out above them.

As soon as it did so Andy pulled his own ripcord and, as his parachute opened, the two of them drifted down together.

When they hit the ground Andy quickly disentangled himself from his parachute and rushed across to where Maurizio lay, still unconscious, amidst the shrouds of his canopy.

Meanwhile the Hercules had radioed details of the emergency to the services below and an ambulance was already racing to the spot where the two men had landed.

"He's still unconscious," cried Andy to the medical team when they arrived.

"Don't worry, we'll have him to hospital in a flash," said one of the team reassuringly.

Hours, and weeks, later the drama had a very happy ending. Hours later Maurizio Brambilla woke up in hospital. He had no broken bones and only a slight headache. What's more, he had no memory of all that had happened from the moment he hit his head when jumping out of the plane. When he heard the facts he naturally could not thank Andy enough.

Weeks later the story finally reached its completely happy ending when Andy Peckett received the Bronze Medal for bravery from the Royal Humane Society.

"I'm certainly proud of him," said his wife Maggie.

"Me too," agreed Maurizio Brambilla, "and more than grateful!"

Notes

Follow up themes: courage; friends; danger.

The following prayer could end the service:

Let us think this morning about all those people whose courage is an inspiration to us all. Let us give thanks for people like Andy whose bravery and quick thinking save the lives of others regularly throughout the world. Amen.

38
What's behind you?

Out of sight, out of mind is a catch phrase firmly rejected by the hero of this story who had the courage and resourcefulness to investigate a 'disappearance'.

Dave Willis hummed as he drove along. The Flamstead End Relief Road in Cheshunt, Hertfordshire was rarely busy at this time and he enjoyed the break from the heavy traffic of the A10 and M25. Glancing in his rear view mirror he saw only one other vehicle – a Ford Sierra, some distance away.

The seconds ticked away and the busy roundabout came into sight ahead as Dave again glanced into the mirror. The Sierra had gone. Making sure it was not alongside and in the blind spot of the mirror he gazed again at the empty road behind.

"Where on earth can it have gone?" Dave muttered to himself. "Nowhere to pull off, nowhere to cross to the other side, it hasn't gone past ..."

With these thoughts pouring through his head Dave reached the roundabout, went round it and headed back up the relief road to try and solve the mystery. Going very slowly he looked across to see if there were any clues to the Sierra's disappearance. Eventually he came across a patch of bushes which looked as if they just might have been disturbed recently.

"Let's have a look," Dave thought as he pulled up his vehicle and went to investigate.

Parting the bushes Dave looked through the undergrowth and quickly found the Sierra which had crashed into a tree. The driver, a young woman, was slumped unconscious over the wheel. From the damage Dave could see that her legs were trapped. All the car doors were jammed so there was little he could do to try and free her. Scrambling back through the thick bushes Dave dashed for his vehicle and quickly alerted the emergency services on his mobile phone.

When they arrived it took the fire brigade and ambulance men two hours to free Stephanie Norris, the trapped driver of the Sierra. She was then rushed to hospital to recover from her injuries.

"Mr Willis saved my life," she said later. "The bushes had closed in after I went through them and my car could have stayed there for days before anybody found it. If he hadn't taken the trouble to come back and look ..."

Notes

Follow up themes: taking the trouble to help others; leaving things to somebody else; 'It'll be all right'.

A useful address for follow up work on this story (and indeed all 'accident' themes) is: Royal Society for the Prevention of Accidents, Cannon House, The Priory, Queensway, Birmingham B4 6BS.
An obvious Bible link here is with the Good Samaritan (Luke 10).

Concluding prayer:
Let us think this morning about giving help when it is needed. Let us remember that giving help often means giving a great deal of time and effort. We pray that we would never be found wanting if our help was needed in any way. Amen.

39
Teamwork

This morning's story starts with the account of a road accident, and then tells of how hundreds of people, thousands of miles away helped the victim.

The boy was four years old. He had already walked hundreds of miles hoping to find a safe place to live. He was sure that both of his parents were dead.

He was still walking. Ahead of him and around him walked, limped and staggered hundreds of other people of all ages. The scorching sun burned down on them and each footstep kicked up a puff of dust. These separate puffs joined to make a dust cloud which hung in the air around the endless line of trudging figures.

This was Rwanda, 1994, and thousands of people were trying to escape from the violence of their country, and find a home somewhere else. Their only means of doing so was to walk ... and walk ... and walk.

The four year old boy was called Nkesha. His feet hurt and he was tired, hungry and thirsty. Sometimes he didn't feel quite so tired but he was always hungry and thirsty.

Suddenly there was a shout at the head of the line.

"The lorries are coming!"

This was followed by a ragged cheer. Lorries usually meant two things and they were both good. The first was possible food supplies; the second was that they might provide lifts for the many walkers and take them to refugee camps.

"How many of them?"

"Can't see yet for the dust."

"Enough to give us all a lift?"

"Still can't … there are only two or three."

At this point panic broke out amongst the walkers. There couldn't be enough food and there certainly would not be enough room for all to get a lift. Perhaps they'd never get out of this terrible country … it might be a case of the first to get to the lorries would be the only ones saved.

So a great pushing and running and surging started up. People were knocked over and shouts and screams filled the air. Nkesha was terrified. Being tiny he couldn't really see what was happening and everybody round him seemed to have gone mad. Putting his arms tightly round his body he crouched down in amongst the shouting, pushing throng.

Meanwhile the lorry drivers, seeing that there was going to be trouble, decided to accelerate away from the main crowd. With roaring engines they picked up speed and on every side people scattered out of their way. The confused and terrified Nkesha still didn't know what was happening until suddenly the crowd in front of him threw themselves to the side of the road and there was a lorry heading straight for him. He had no chance to get out of the way … suddenly everything went black after he felt a terrible blow on the head.

Meanwhile a British press photographer, who had been walking with the group and taking pictures, saw what had happened.

Flinging his cameras round his neck he dashed over to the injured boy, calling for help as he did so. Others rushed to his aid. It was obvious that Nkesha was badly hurt and needed immediate care and attention. Red Cross workers were soon on the scene and he was expertly treated.

Hours later on a warm August evening in Great Britain, millions of viewers switched their TV sets on to watch the 10 o'clock news. Within minutes there was the story and photographs of Nkesha's accident taking place thousands of miles away in Africa.

"How terrible."

"Poor little boy."

"He's only four years old."

"What can we do to help?"

Comments like these filled houses up and down the country and the telephone lines to TV News at Ten were jammed. Later on, a spokesman for the programme said that it was the biggest response they had ever had for any item on News Ten. Everybody just wanted to help in any way they could.

Notes

Follow up themes: third world themes; the Red Cross; communications.

The Red Cross hoped to help by finding a place for Nkesha in a Zairian orphanage. For related support resource/information a useful address is: The British Red Cross Society, 9 Grosvenor Crescent, London SW1X 7ES.

Another useful source is: Christian Aid, PO Box 1, London SW9 8BH.

There is a Bible reference which takes reflections on this story one step further and could promote much thought for discussion. It might also be used in a prayer context whilst concluding this service.

Is there a man among you who will offer his son a stone when he asks for bread, or a snake when he asks for fish? *Matthew 7:9*

40
Carelessness costs lives

This morning's story is about taking care – and the dreadful things which can happen when people are careless.

Sunday 25th August 1861 was a bright, sunny day.

"Oh what I would give to be home in bed, or even in a deck chair in the garden," thought Henry Killick to himself. Henry was a signal man who worked in a signal box on the London to Brighton railway line. On this August day he had been on duty for twenty four hours non-stop, far far longer that he should have been.

Meanwhile at Brighton Station there was great excitement. Lots of people were looking forward to a day out.

"Where are you going?"

"Up to London for the day."

"Lots of trains going up there today."

"I know, there's two excursions."

"And the regular service."

"It's exciting, but I always get a bit scared when were have to go through that Clayton tunnel."

In 1861 trips on trains were very popular, and nearly all the trains which travelled on Sundays were full of people enjoying themselves. Many of these travellers were still rather nervous of being trapped in long, dark tunnels, and the Clayton tunnel was certainly a long one! Henry Killick's signal box was at the Brighton end of it.

As quickly as possible the London bound trains were loaded up at Brighton station. Train A was a sixteen-coach excursion train, Train B was a seventeen-coach excursion train and Train C was the regular Brighton to London twelve-coach train. The timetable said that there should be a gap of 25 minutes between the departure of each train – yet all three trains left within seven minutes of each other.

So, already, very careless mistakes had been made, and more were to follow.

Train A reached the Clayton tunnel and roared inside. This should have set off the automatic signal to Danger to show following trains that it was not safe to enter the tunnel yet. The signal did not work so an alarm bell rang in Henry's signal box to tell him this.

"Got to act quickly," said the desperately tired Henry to himself, and immediately sent a 'train in tunnel' message to the signal box at the other end of the tunnel. Then to his horror he looked up ...

"Oh no," he cried.

The second train from Brighton was now hurtling towards his end of the Clayton tunnel. There was only one thing to do. Picking up a red Danger flag, Henry scrambled outside and waved it frantically at the onrushing train. It flashed past and Henry wondered agonisingly if the driver had seen ...

"I must find out as quickly as possible," he thought. Running back into the signal box he sent another message to the signal box at the northern end of the Clayton.

"Is the tunnel clear?" was Henry's message.

Just as this message was being received in the northern signal box Train A came steaming out of the tunnel.

"Tunnel clear," flashed the message back to Henry.

But it wasn't!

Driver Scott of Train B had seen the red flag of Henry's danger signal. Unable to stop quickly his train had rushed a long way into the tunnel before the brakes took. Then, to see what was wrong Driver Scott began reversing his train – backwards towards the entrance of the tunnel.

Meanwhile Train C was approaching the southern end of the Clayton. This time Henry thought he was prepared.

"The signal is not working, but I know from the message I've just received that the tunnel is clear. Therefore I'll wave the white flag at the driver to tell him everything is OK."

So, as Train C thundered towards the tunnel Henry waved the white flag telling the driver that the line was clear. Just minutes later the onrushing Train C smashed into the reversing Train B and many, many people were killed.

An investigation into the crash was held and all the carelessness and mistakes were discovered – too late for the many people who were killed or injured.

Notes

Follow up themes: responsibility; care/carelessness.

This is an assembly where the use of a few diagrams, prepared in advance, can greatly enhance the telling of the story.

The following prayer could be used to conclude the service:

Let us pray this morning for all those people who:
   drive buses
   drive lorries
   drive trains
   steer ships
   pilot aeroplanes.

Let us pray for all those people who work hard to keep all kinds of transport safe for passengers to use. Let us give thanks for their skill, experience and sense of responsibility. Amen.

For those interested in following up this story in other relevant areas then a useful address is The Royal Society for the Prevention of Accidents, Cannon House, The Priory, Queensway, Birmingham B4 6BS.

41
Help!

Someone once said that the worst peace is better than the best war. War is a most terrible time yet sometimes it produces remarkable stories.

In 1943, during the Second World War, the greatest tank battle the world had ever seen was taking place at a place called Kursk in Russia. The Russians were finally driving the German invaders out of their country … but they might not succeed if they did not win this battle.

Evgeny Shkurdalor was the commander of the 5th Russian Guards army and he led his men from the turret of a tank.

"Remember," he went on, "we've got to keep pressing forward all the time, no matter what happens. If we win this battle we can win the war."

So the great battle went on, week after week over an area of hundreds of square miles. One day Evgeny's tank was rolling forward when a shell hit it. Instantly the tank caught fire and the crew dragged their badly wounded commander to safety.

"We can't stay here," said one of them.

"We've got to get the commander to a doctor quickly, or he'll die," shouted another.

"Look there's a lorry going back to base, stop it quickly."

The tired and dazed soldiers managed to stop the lorry and the bleeding and unconscious commander was loaded on board. With every jolt and bump worsening his wounds the lorry ground back to the area where the wounded were being treated. Finally it arrived at a field hospital.

"We've got a desperately wounded man here," cried two of the soldiers as they carried Evgeny as carefully, but as fast as they could. "He needs help urgently."

A quiet voice spoke calmly to them. "Put him on that stretcher."

The soldier, surprised to hear a woman's voice, looked round and saw a slim, but tired looking woman doctor with a stethoscope dangling round her neck. Carefully they lowered Evgeny onto the stretcher.

The doctor, whose name was Olga Borisenko, began to examine the pale, bloodstained figure after trying to stop the blood flowing from his wounds. She looked up anxiously. "Orderly, this man needs a blood transfusion immediately. Get some blood at once."

Just as the orderly was about to turn away another doctor, who was nearby and had heard what was going on, held up his hand.

"Don't bother my man. We've had so many wounded that there is no blood for any more transfusions."

"But he'll die I tell you," Olga snapped tensely.

"Well then I'm afraid ..." began the doctor, when Olga interrupted again.

"Very well," she said firmly. "Orderly bring that other stretcher over here."

Puzzled, the group wondered what was going to happen. They didn't have to wait long to find out. Olga lay down on the second stretcher herself.

"Well, come on," she said to the other doctor, "he needs blood, doesn't he – so take some of mine."

So with the battle raging around them this courageous doctor gave some of her own blood to the badly wounded officer.

The story had a happy ending. Evgeny Shkurdalov recovered from his wounds and when he heard how he had been saved he sought out Dr Borisenko to thank her for saving his life. As the war finally drew to a close they saw more and more of each other and finally got married.

Notes

Follow up themes: doctors and nurses; war; peace; health.

The battle of Kursk in 1943 lasted for seven weeks and was fought over an area the size of Wales. The casualties were horrific: 254,000 Russians were killed and 608,000 were wounded. The Germans lost 100,000 men killed. The German defeat was the beginning of the end of their Russian campaign.

The following prayer might be used:

No matter how inspiring stories which come from wartime situations are, let us pray this morning for peace in every part of the world. In doing so let us remember the words of a very old prayer:

Lord, help us to remember that we are the children of the universe, no less than the trees and the stars. Give us the wisdom to be careful and happy to pray endlessly for peace because, despite its pain and disappointments, this is still a beautiful world. Amen.

(The last part of this prayer is adapted from one written in 1692.)

42
Buried alive

Being a miner has always been a hard, dangerous job. This is the story of one miner's incredible courage and determination.

If you go down a working coal mine, walk or crawl along a narrow seam, and then put out your light, the darkness is absolutely complete. Think about this as you listen to this morning's story ...

Jack was hard at work hacking coal from the rock face in front of him. Hundreds of feet below ground, he and his friends were half way through their shift.

"Are you playing football on Saturday, Jack?" called out Bob, working a few feet away.

"Yeah – should be a good match too."

"Football – bah, I'll be glad to be back to my pigeons," called out another miner working nearby.

Then, cutting across the noise of all work and conversation, came the sound all miners dread. The thunderous roar of stone falling filled the air, dust rushed through the seam like a choking blanket and terrible cries of pain echoed along the shaft.

When the terrible noise stopped Jack was conscious of several things.

"I'm not hurt," he thought, "not even a scratch, but I'd better see who is – and then we'll have to get out of here quickly."

Raising his miner's lamp to peer through the swirling dust Jack then saw a sight which sent a chill running right through him.

Directly ahead of him, where the seam stretched back to the shaft entrance and where Bob and all his other friends had been working, there was just a solid, terrible mass of fallen rock. There was absolutely no way through it – he was trapped!

Meanwhile in the rest of the pit news of the accident spread like wildfire and rescuers rushed to the scene.

"There's been an enormous fall of rock," said one.

"I'm afraid many men have been killed."

"Do you think any could be trapped?"

"We'll start digging in as soon as we can."

"Start tapping to see if anyone taps back."

The rescue work began. The roof was carefully shored up as men tried to get through the fallen stone to rescue any miners who had survived.

Day after day went by until finally the manager said to a crowd of distressed people on the surface of the pit, "I'm desperately sorry but we're sure there's nobody left alive down there."

He was wrong. Jack was alive, alone and in pitch darkness now that his lamp had long since gone out. As hour after hour passed by he waited and hoped, chewing bits of bark from a fallen pit prop, and moistening his tongue with a damp finger after running it over some wet rock.

Eventually he knew that the rescuers thought that everybody caught in the disaster was dead. Days had already gone by, but he was still breathing so there was air getting into his tiny space in the rocks somewhere.

"If there's air getting in here, all I've got to do is follow the draught and get out," thought Jack to himself.

So, in complete darkness and surrounded by rocks, the determined miner began to feel for the tiny holes through which the draught was coming. Then, chipping at them to make them bigger, and tearing at them with his bare hands, he sought desperately to make a space big enough to crawl through.

Day and night he worked, falling into an exhausted sleep from time to time. The draught was his only hope and, very, very, gradually it began to get stronger and the rocks began to thin out. Then, miraculously, Jack broke through into another disused mine seam which led back to the main shaft.

Exhausted, starving, desperately thirsty, his clothes in rags and his finger nails torn and bleeding, the determined miner collapsed into the arms of a group of his fellow workers coming along the shaft.

"It's Jack!"

"It can't be."

"It is I tell you – and he's alive."

"Let's get him to the surface quickly – he needs a doctor quick!"

"But it's nine days since that fall of stone!"

Jack was rushed to the surface of the pit and taken to hospital. There he made a full recovery and was soon back at work.

Notes

This event took place in the South East Durham coal field many years ago – perhaps near the turn of the century. It was told to the author by a veteran miner and one of its more memorable aspects was that Jack arrived at the pit head just as his funeral was being organised in the village.

Follow up themes: fortitude, determination, loneliness.

Concluding Prayer:

Let us think this morning about ourselves. Let us pray that if we are ever in a difficult situation alone we will have the courage and determination to deal with it in the best way we can. Let us give thanks for the gifts of mind and body which we have been given. Amen.

43
Hearing dogs

Animals who help us is always a popular topic and 'hearing' dogs for the deaf are an inspiring example.

7th April 1983 was a very important day for Mr and Mrs Chapman. They travelled to London to be given a dog, and dozens of newspaper reporters, TV reporters and photographers were there to see them get it. You see, he wasn't just a pet, because Mr and Mrs Chapman were deaf and their new dog was going to 'hear' for them.

Training hearing dogs for deaf people began in 1982. For a start the dogs had to be chosen carefully and only those which were intelligent, calm and friendly were selected for training.

"Now," said the trainers when they planned their programmes, "what are the important noises deaf people need to be aware of?"

Everyone had a suggestion to make.

"The door bell ringing."

"A baby crying in another room."

"A kettle whistling to show it is boiling!"

"An alarm clock going off."

So a list of these important noises was built up and the training of the dogs began. They were taught to listen for certain noises and then, when they heard them, go to their owner, tap him with their paw, and draw attention to the noise and where it was coming from.

As you can imagine this work needed a great deal of care and patience from the trainer and the dogs had to work very, very, hard. Eventually it was found that they could be trained to do the job in about four months. After that they were ready to work with their new owners.

Since 1983 many deaf people have become very grateful for their four legged 'hearing' partners!

Notes

Follow up themes: animals who help us; senses; handicaps.

There are many specific follow ups to this particular theme:
Make a list of important noises associated with various rooms in the house which it might be important for a hearing dog to be aware of. Apart from help with sounds, why else might a deaf person appreciate having such a dog? How does having a hearing dog improve the quality of life of a person who is deaf?

Useful address: Hearing Dogs for the Deaf Training Centre, Chinnor, Oxon OX9 4BA.

Concluding prayer:
Let us pray this morning for people who are handicapped in any way. Let us give thanks for the skill and wisdom of other human beings, and animals, who help to make life less difficult, and more enjoyable for these unfortunate people. Amen.

44
Sep's story

All over the country there are old people living alone. It is sometimes easy to forget how determined and courageous some of them are.

Sep lived alone. He had done so for 27 years, ever since his wife died. Sep was 88 years old.

"I started work on my fourteenth birthday, down the pit pushing tub," he told me once. "It was pitch dark down there, and we didn't have time for lunch breaks – I carried my sandwiches in a tin round my neck and ate them when I could."

One early summer's morning Sep finished his morning cleaning of the house and was about to start making his dinner.

"Aah," he thought, "that fire looks pretty low. I'd better go up the yard and chop some sticks."

Going up the long concrete back yard of his house, he laid a piece of wood over an upturned bucket and began to chop it. Suddenly, one of his feet slipped, the axe flew out of his hands and he fell onto his side. A searing, breath taking pain shot through his hip – and he couldn't get up.

"It's no good shouting. There's nobody to hear me," thought the old man. "I can't lie here for ever because nobody's due to come until the milkman in the morning. There's only one thing for it – I'll have to crawl to the telephone."

Gritting his teeth, he began the long slow crawl down the concrete yard. Every movement sent more pain shooting through his body and sweat poured from his forehead. Inch by inch he got nearer to the steps leading to the back door, the passage and the telephone.

For one and half hours the old man levered himself along in slow pain-filled progress. Finally he reached the telephone. Even then he didn't panic.

"Mrs Jones," he said quietly after ringing one of his neighbours' number. "I've got a little bit of a problem. Could you possibly spare a minute to come over?"

Sensing the urgency of the situation despite the old man's calm message, Mrs Jones was with him shortly. She instantly called 999 and within half an hour an ambulance had arrived.

"Sorry to be a nuisance lads," said Sep to the ambulance men, still convinced that he was rather wasting people's time!

"You just take it easy and we'll have you sorted out in a crack," said one of the men cheerfully.

Soon they, and Sep, were on the way to hospital. There he had an emergency operation to replace his hip which was broken so badly it couldn't be repaired.

"He's a remarkable man," said the doctor. "To spend an hour and a half crawling with such an injury shows how determined he is – not to mention tough!"

These events happened eighteen months ago and Sep still lives alone, chops wood, drives his small car and tells a joke to anybody who will listen!

Notes

Follow up themes: old age; loneliness; good neighbours.

Useful address: St John's Ambulance, 1 Grosvenor Crescent, London SW1 7EH. (A useful source of information for what to do with accident cases etc.)

Concluding prayer:

Let us pray this morning for all old people wherever they may be. We pray that they be given comfort in loneliness, strength in difficulties and hope when they are in need. Amen

45
HMS Birkenhead

Such was the courage and discipline of the young soldiers on the sinking ship that for more than a hundred years 'the Birkenhead drill' has been a phrase denoting bravery.

"She's hit a rock!"

The cry spread through the ship like wildfire. The year was 1852. HMS Birkenhead was on her way to South Africa full of fresh new soldiers going to reinforce British regiments there. The captain had unwisely steered the old paddle steamer too close to the deadly rocks near the Cape of Good Hope. More cries sounded in the cool night air.

"She's taking water too fast! No chance of saving her!"

"Get ready to abandon ship!"

700 soldiers, along with women and small children, were crammed on board and as water poured into cabins there was every chance of panic. Then one of the senior army officers had an idea.

"Sound the bugle for parade!" he shouted.

Instantly buglers summoned the soldiers to parade, and within minutes they were lined up to attention on the deck of the ship.

As the water swirled round their feet, then their ankles, then their knees, the soldiers stood silently and watched as women and children were loaded into the too few lifeboats. As the ship groaned and heaved the water crept hungrily up the legs of the 700 men standing in long silent ranks.

Finally an officer's voice sounded above the chaos. "There are no lifeboats, men, and the ship's going down. The shore is not too far away so you'll have to swim for it. Good luck – jump now."

The ranks of soldiers moved forward and the young men jumped into the boiling sea. Sadly many could not swim and others were caught in thick seaweed and drowned. Only 184 out of the 700 made it safely ashore.

Notes

Follow up themes: courage; sacrifice; discipline.

HMS Birkenhead was holed at 2 am in the morning. What made the heroic story even more impressive was that many of the soldiers were very young indeed and had only been in the army a few weeks.

Biblical reference: There is no greater love than this, that a man should lay down his life for his friends. *John 15:13*

Concluding prayer:

Let us give thanks this morning for the inspiration of brave people who, throughout history, have set the highest examples of how men, women and children can behave. Amen.

46
Train rescue

This is the story of the courage and determination of a young student who rescued his friend from a terrible train crash.

The train pulled out of the small Indian town of Puri. Ahead of it lay the 40 hour journey to Delhi.

"I'm glad we're going home at last," said Nikko Metherell.

"Me too" replied Tony Danesi.

The two students settled down in their sleeping compartment and chatted about the last two months, during which they had backpacked all over India. They were now heading to Delhi to fly back home to England.

Hour after hour the train rumbled along the track. Friday night passed into Saturday, and then into Sunday. It was 3 o'clock Sunday morning when it happened.

"There's something wrong !" yelled Nikko, waking up with the train rocking madly from side to side. "We're going to crash!"

Suddenly the compartment seemed to be flying through the air, and then bouncing down an embankment. The carriage behind crashed with a terrible noise on top of it and everywhere the scream of breaking metal was mixed with the shouts and cries of terrified passengers.

Nikko, battered and bruised, looked up to where the roof had been torn off the carriage and climbed up out of it. He could see that Tony was much more badly hurt, but needed help to get him out.

"Here," he called out, "over here."

People from a nearby village were running across the fields to help. Two of them helped Nikko drag the badly injured Tony from the wreck.

"Don't worry, don't worry, we'll soon have you as good as new," muttered Nikko as he bandaged Tony's badly cut arm with some clothing. Then with a villager's help he carried Tony on a bed which was being used as a stretcher away from the wreck. Sometime later Nikko got his friend an ambulance which was going to the nearest town, a place called Agra.

"I still think he might need my help," thought Nikko and after being given a pair of shoes by a complete stranger he hitch hiked to Agra and found Tony again in a student hospital.

"He's just not getting better," Nikko said when, after a number of telephone calls he managed to get an ambulance to take Tony to a better hospital in Delhi. There once again he waited by his friend's side until an air lift to Singapore could be arranged. By now Tony's father had flown out from England to help and Tony's injuries began to heal.

"There is no doubt whatsoever," said the Dansi family, "Nikko saved Tony's life."

Notes

Follow up themes: friendship; disasters; emergency services.

This incident took place during India's worst ever train crash. In August 1995 a train hit some stray cattle on the line near Firozabad, 200 miles south east of Delhi. A second train, which Nikko and Tony were travelling in, then ploughed into the first one and of 1,200 passengers some 500 were killed.

One of the reasons Nikko was able to get help was because he telephoned his grandmother in England and she alerted the British Embassy in Delhi.

Concluding prayer:

Let us pray this morning for all those who are travelling on land, at sea or in the air. We pray that their journey may be safe and that they all reach their destination unharmed. Amen.

47
Missing

Sometimes unexpected events in our own lives give us an insight into what it must be like to be very lonely and desperately poor.

Jim was tired. He was making a long journey by aeroplane to another country and things had not gone very well. For a start he had had to change airports when he started the journey and this had meant a long and expensive taxi ride. Then his plane had been delayed and now it was late at night, and here he was at a strange airport feeling weary and grubby.

"Well, it will be all right when I get my case," thought Jim. "Then I'll have the keys to the flat that I'm staying in and I can get out there and have a good wash and sleep."

So Jim stood under a big sign which said 'Luggage from Flt 610 here' and watched as the conveyor belt began to fill up with cases. Slowly it went round and round and the other passengers lifted off their luggage as it reached them. Getting more worried Jim looked anxiously for his case ... but eventually he realised that all the other passengers and luggage had gone. He was alone in the large hall with the empty conveyor belt going round in front of him. His case was lost!

For another minute Jim just stood there. He realised he had no clothes except the ones he stood up in. Even his toothbrush was in his case. The keys to the flat he was supposed to be going to were also in the missing luggage, so he couldn't go there. It was very late at night and he couldn't speak a word of the language of the country he was in.

Suddenly Jim felt very lonely indeed.

Now this story had a happy ending. When Jim reported the loss of his case someone was found who could speak English. Even though it was very late he was found somewhere to stay for the night – and his case arrived by a later flight the next day. But just for a few moments that night Jim had realised what it must be like to have no friends or family, and to be desperately lonely and have no home.

Notes

Follow up themes: loneliness; poverty; being lost in various ways.

Many children are now experienced air travellers and there is considerable discussion potential leading on from this story in considering the many people, and the organisation required, for safe and trouble-free journeys to take place. Such journeys might then be compared with those which took place in Biblical settings: the Good Samaritan, and the journey of Joseph and Mary before Jesus was born.

Concluding prayer:

Let us give thanks this morning for all those who look after travellers. Let us also pray for those whose journey through life is made difficult by loneliness, hardship, poverty and homelessness. Let us pray that these people are given help. Amen.

48
What's in a road name?

This is a story of self sacrifice commemorated fifty years later in the naming of a new road.

What is the street where you live called? Do you know how it got its name? There are some very interesting stories behind the names of streets and roads. Here is one of them.

In the busy town of Cheshunt, just north of London, a relief road was built to take traffic away from the main streets. For some time this was just called 'the Relief Road' until the members of Broxbourne Council met to give it a name.

"I think we should give this road a name which really means something to the people who live here," said Councillor Don Smith.

"I agree," replied another councillor. "We all do," said the rest.

The councillors then discussed something which had happened just over fifty years ago, in the dark days of the Second World War ...

The engines of the Liberator bomber screamed as they tried to keep the aeroplane in the sky. It was a cloudy August day in 1944 and the aircraft was one of the 577 US Airforce Bomber Group which had been flying on a raid to Cherbourg in France. Bad weather had forced the group to turn back and in doing so the Liberator had collided with a B-17 Flying Fortress. Now, badly damaged, it was struggling to return to base.

"I can't hold her much longer," gasped the pilot, Second Lieutenant Ellis, over the intercom.

Around the battered plane the tired and shaken crew listened to the struggling engines.

"Where are we now?" queried Ellis suddenly.

"Just coming up to a place called Cheshunt," replied the navigator.

"She's going ..." shouted the pilot, seeing the rows of houses below. "I must try and hold her until we reach those fields in the distance ..."

On the ground below hundreds of people gazed up at the stricken bomber as it lurched and roared over the rooftops. They could almost feel the pilot fighting the controls to keep it in the air long enough to miss the houses.

"Prepare for crash landing," cried Lt Ellis as the Liberator skimmed over the last row of houses and sank towards a field ahead.

Sadly, and to the horror of those people watching, Lt Ellis's great skill was not quite enough and, as the plane hit the ground it exploded. The brave pilot and all his crew were killed in the crash ...

Now, when motorists drive along the road which cuts through the fields where the Liberator crashed all those years ago, they can be reminded of the courage and self sacrifice of a brave man when they look at the name of the road ... Lieutenant Ellis Way.

Notes

Follow up themes: thought for others; war and peace.

At the time of the crash grateful residents set up a plaque to commemorate the Liberator crew's heroism. This is now in Cheshunt library, and reads: "To the valiant American airmen who, on August 12th, 1944, sacrificed their lives to prevent their aircraft from crashing onto our homes."

An appropriate Biblical reference is:
There is no greater love than this, that a man should lay down his life for his friends.

Concluding prayer:
Let us think this morning about this sad and moving story. Let us give thanks for those remarkable people who are so brave that they are prepared to give their own lives so that others might be saved. Let us pray also for the end of war everywhere so that brave men are never called upon to fight each other. Let us pray finally for our own town or village. Amen.

49
The entertainer

'Great moments come to every man' – and it is particularly pleasing when they come to someone less fortunate that most.

John was a piano tuner, and he was also blind. He tuned the pianos for many schools and he often got invitations to their concerts. One day he was in a head teacher's office.

"Next Friday night we're having a concert for the parents, John. There's going to be singing by the choir, poetry readings and a slide show of last term's school trip. Will you come along and be our guest?"

"Thank you," replied John, "we'd be delighted to, wouldn't we, Jess?" As he said this John bent forward and ruffled the ears of his guide dog Jess.

The evening of the concert arrived. It was winter and dark early, but the school hall looked lovely with children's paintings decorating the walls. The place was packed with about three hundred parents and friends there. Many of the adults were standing behind the chairs at the back and there was a great feeling of excitement in the air. Along with the other invited guests, John and Jess were sitting in the front row next to the headmistress.

Soon the concert got under way but then, after about ten minutes, something happened – all the lights went out!

"It's a power cut," groaned somebody, as the singers stopped in mid song.

For a moment or two there was just a hint of panic in the air and then the head teacher spoke up.

"Will everybody please stay exactly where they are. Mr Black will go to the caretaker's house and we'll see about getting some emergency lighting."

Some of the children were still quite frightened. But until the head teacher spoke John had no idea what he happened because of course he couldn't tell whether the lights were on or not! Then he had an idea …

"Mrs Whiting," he whispered.

The head teacher listened to what he had to say and then spoke again. "Ladies and gentlemen, we're not sure how long it will be before we get some lights but until then our good friend John is going to entertain us."

Jess and John made their way to the piano and John ran his hands over the keys. He was a wonderful pianist and of course he didn't need music or light to play. Soon the whole hall was enraptured by his playing. The darkness seemed to add to the joy of the music, and then John played well known songs that everybody could sing.

After about a quarter of an hour the caretaker arrived with a big torch and he stood at the back of the hall and shone it on John so it almost seemed as if the blind pianist was floodlit. When the lights finally came back on everybody in the hall stood up and gave John a tremendous round of applause. It was a night neither he nor they ever forgot.

Notes

Follow up themes: handicaps; joy; great moments.

The full quotation which is relevant to this story is: Great moments come to every man, some situation where he can, attain such fame that folks acclaim the very mention of his name." *(Source unknown)*

Two useful addresses here could be:
Guide dogs for the Blind, 9-11 Park St., Windsor, Berks. SL4 1JR.
Royal Institute for the Blind, 224 Great Portland Street, London W1.

Concluding Prayer:
Let us give thanks this morning for the joy that is bought to us by music. Let us give thanks for musicians everywhere, and particularly those who are physically handicapped but still give other people so much pleasure. Amen.

50
Boy alone

When we think of the things which make us feel secure, the following story illustrates the desperate situation war causes.

Tien Chi listened carefully.

"It's no good," his grandfather was saying. "It's all because of the war. The new government are going to take away our land and that is all there is to it."

"But how can we live?" Tien Chi's mother asked anxiously. "Without that tiny bit of land to grow food we'll starve."

Tien Chi was only ten years old, but he had got used to hearing bad news. When the war had broken out in his country his father had been called away to fight – and he could still remember the dreadful day when news came that he had been killed.

After that Tien Chi and his mother had moved back to live with his grandparents. They had just about managed to stay alive on the food his grandfather had grown ... now this. Tien Chi's thought were interrupted by his mother's voice.

"I can make a little money selling things at the market," she said.

"But we've got to get away from this country and find somewhere else to live. Then we might have a better life."

"You're right," replied Grandfather, "but the only way we can do that is by buying a place on one of the refugee boats that try to make it to other countries."

"Well, we've got a tiny bit of money saved up," went on Tien Chi's mother, "but it's only enough for one person on the boat. If they go first, the rest of us will have to follow when we've got more money."

"Well, who is going to go first?" muttered Grandmother.

Tien Chi felt a prickle of awful fear run down his back as all eyes turned on him. "But ..." he began.

It was no use. This was the only way the family thought it could survive. A week later Tien Chi, his mother and grandparents stood at the dock side. Bobbing in the water alongside the dock was an old, dirty, ragged looking boat. Packed on its deck were people of all ages, clasping little bundles and looking miserable and afraid.

"Come on," shouted the thin, mean looking captain. "Everybody who is going get on board."

Tien Chi hugged his mother desperately one last time and then stepped down onto the crowded, swaying boat. Nobody knew where the boat was going to, or when it would reach a safe place. Would he ever see his mother or grandparents again?

Tien Chi had never felt so alone in his life.

(This story is based on the experiences of Nguyen Van Tai, a ten year old Vietnamese boy. After nine dreadful days at sea in 1980 his boat was picked up by a British tanker and the refugees were taken first to Thailand and then, ultimately to Great Britain.)

Notes

Follow up themes: families; alone; hardships.

The following Bible quotation could be useful in the context of people like Tien Chi being 'tested':

"In dealing with man it is God's purpose to test them and to see what they truly are." *Ecclesiastes 3:18*

Concluding prayer:

Let us pray this morning for those children, wherever they may be in the world, who through war or some other disaster, lose their houses and families. Let us pray that they may be given courage, faith and hope. Amen.

III

Christian stories

51
The joke?

When is a joke not a joke? Matthew found this out when he tried a trick on a blind man.

Matthew was young – and always ready for a practical joke.

"Here he comes," he said to himself. "I'm going to enjoy this."

Matthew stood quite still and watched the familiar figure walking towards him. He knew the blind preacher very well. Every day the blind old man walked slowly over the countryside paths he knew so well to preach to groups of eager listeners. He got nearer.

"Morning, Father," called out Matthew.

"Good morning, my son," answered the blind man, who was known as the Venerable Bede.

"I've got a message for you, Father," went on the secretly grinning boy. "There's a crowd of people about half a mile away. They asked me to look out for you and take you to them. They've come to listen to you preach."

"Very well … er … what's your name?"

"Matthew."

"Very well Matthew, lead me to them."

The boy took the old monk's hand and led him across some fields, away from the usual familiar paths. Eventually they reached a bleak and stony clearing.

"We're here sir," said the boy. "Your audience is just waiting for you to speak, they're waiting for you in silence."

As he spoke his grin grew wider. The wind whistled through the hawthorn bushes, but, as for human beings, there wasn't one in sight. What a lark this was going to be! Here was the great blind preacher going to speak to what he thought was a great big crowd – and there was nobody there! Matthew could hardly contain his laughter.

Then the old monk began to speak. Set against the background of the piercing wind and the fluffy clouds sweeping across the empty sky, his voice rang out clearly, and with never a word too many. He told of the wonders and beauty of the world; he reminded the lonely countryside round him of the birth of Jesus; he praised the kindness of generous and thoughtful men.

Standing to one side, Matthew listened.

"I wonder what he'll say when I tell him there's nobody here," he thought with a smirk. "One certain fact, as soon as I've told him I'm going to run off – and quick."

But as the old monk's words rang through the country air Matthew began to listen to them more carefully. Then, as suddenly as he had started speaking, the Bede stopped. For a second there was silence and then a great swell of noise arose, as if a thousand people were speaking at once.

"Amen ... Amen ... Amen Venerable Bede."

"What ..." cried Matthew, astonished and rather frightened at the same time. Where were they, all these people, where could they hide here? Then he realised that the voices were coming from every stone, every blade of grass, every berry and branch.

The noise stopped. The boy and the monk stood alone. Instinctively the boy dropped to his knees.

"Amen," he said. "Father, forgive me."

Then he led the blind man back to his monastery.

Notes

Follow up themes: jokes; mystery; awe; disabilities.

The Venerable Bede was a monk who lived in a monastery in the north east of England. Through diligent study he became one of the most learned men in Europe. Excessive use of his eyes in dimly lit cells caused him to go blind, but even when so afflicted he continued to dictate books, and go out into the neighbourhood to preach.

Prayer:

Dear God, Help us to enjoy life by sharing jokes and laughter with as many people as we can. Keep us always however from the cruelty of laughing at the misfortune of others. Amen.

52
A Christian mystery

The early Christians were brave and often daring men and women. They had to take many different kinds of chances.

In the history of the early Christian Church there is one story to which we don't know the ending. We do know however how things should have worked out ...

The two men sat in the prison cell. One was old, worn and tired, the other young and strong. The old man laid his hand on his young friend's shoulder and spoke in a firm voice.

"Tomorrow you will be released – you know what you have to do."

"Yes Paul," replied Onesimus. "I must return to my master in Colossae and ask him to forgive me."

"That you must," went on Paul, "but you will have a long letter from me which I hope will help."

The two men were in prison in Rome. Paul was the great Christian missionary who was spreading the word about Jesus throughout the Roman Empire. Unfortunately a great fire had broken out in Rome, the Christians were blamed for it, and Paul was one of many who were imprisoned and eventually put to death.

Onesimus on the other hand was a thief. He was a slave from Colossae who had stolen some of his master's property and escaped to Rome. There he had been caught and put in prison. Once in prison Onesimus met Paul, and marvelled at the great Christian's courage and kindness. In return Paul saw in the young Onesimus a man who given another chance could prove honest and trustworthy.

So, despite his own pain and approaching execution, Paul took time to write a long letter to Philemon, Onesimus' master, telling him that his slave had become a Christian and begging him to give Onesimus another chance.

"Please," wrote Paul, "greet him as you would greet me, not as a slave, but as a brother."

We know that, shortly after this, Paul was killed by the Romans – but we do not know what happened to Onesimus when he got back to Colossae. We can only hope that Paul's letter helped Onesimus to freedom and a better life.

Notes

Follow up themes: forgiveness, help.

'Onesimus' means 'useful' – a relevant point to use in any follow up work to do with this story.

Relevant Biblical references to the story are: Paul's letter to Philemon, vv 9-10, 16, 21, 25.

Closing prayer:

Let us think this morning about our mistakes. Let us pray that we may be found worthy of a second chance, as we hope Onesimus was. Amen.

53
A traveller alone

Most of us like to know where we're going when we start a journey – and we like to have family or friends with us.

The group of men stood talking. They looked tired and worried and kept looking nervously around them. This was because they were Christians and had many enemies. Jerusalem especially had become dangerous for them.

"Do you think we are safe here?"

"Safer than in Jerusalem – that's certain."

"Yes, they seem determined to get rid of us Christians once and for all."

One of the men, taller and calmer than the others, had less to say. He stood to one side peering down the long, dusty road. One of the other men called to him.

"Philip – hey, Philip."

"Yes, my friend?"

"Do you think we should stay here?"

"You can if you wish, but I've got another long journey to make."

"Where to?"

"Samaria."

"Samaria! Did you say Samaria?"

"I did. When our Lord left us he said that we should spread his message far and wide. Well I'm going to Samaria to do just that."

"But the Samaritans will kill you. They've always been our enemies, right back to the days of David and Goliath."

"Nevertheless," said Philip. "I must go there."

So Philip set off on the long, long journey to Samaria.

As he walked he thought of all the terrible things which had happened to Christians since Jesus had left them. They had been imprisoned, tortured, driven out of towns. And yet ... the more that happened to them the more their belief seemed to grow, and the more people wanted to hear about it.

"I don't expect it will be like that in Samaria though," thought Philip. "I'd better prepare myself for the worst."

But when Philip got to Samaria he got a tremendous surprise.

"We've heard stories about Jesus," said the people. "Can you tell us more?"

So Philip was treated kindly and welcomed everywhere he went. People flocked from all parts of the country to hear his stories of Jesus, and more and more people became Christians.

When the news of this got back to Judea, Peter and John were full of admiration for Philip.

"He's done a marvellous job in Samaria," said Peter. "How many men could have had the courage to go alone to a land we always thought of as our greatest enemy?"

"Only someone with great courage and great faith could have done it," replied John. "Now we must see that Philip gets help."

So the good news began to spread far and wide.

Notes

Follow up themes: journeys; different kinds of courage; what is 'good news'?

For those who wish to pursue the original source of this story then the Biblical reference is Acts 8: 1-25. The whole theme of the difficulties the early Christians faced is a fruitful area for assembly material. The early Christians' difficulties multiplied after the Ascension of Jesus – Biblical references for this event are Luke 2 and Acts 1.

From another 'inspired traveller', John Wesley, came some words which might be used in prayer at the end of this assembly:

Do all the good you can,
By all the means you can,
In all the ways you can,
In all the places you can,
At all the times you can,
To all the people you can,
As long as ever you can.

54
Beginnings

One of Britain's most magnificent cathedrals is at Durham. This is the story of how it came to be built there.

The band of travelling monks were tired.

"It just won't move," said one of them wearily.

"But why?" asked another.

They were talking about a cart which had a coffin on it. No matter how much the travellers cajoled or threatened the horses pulling the wagon, it just would not move.

"Very well" said the leader of the monks. "We'll rest here for a while and say a prayer for guidance."

Now the body which was in the coffin was that of a very famous monk who had died. His name was St Cuthbert and he had said before his death that the monks would get some guidance as to where to bury him.

So the party ate, drank and rested. They said a quiet prayer and then one of them fell into a deep sleep. The others talked.

"I think the cart won't move because God wants us to bury Cuthbert somewhere near here."

"You must be right, there's no other explanation for it."

"Near here ... but where?"

Just then the sleeping monk awoke. "I've had a dream," he cried. "God wants us to bury Cuthbert at Dunholm."

"Dunholm? Where's Dunholm? Never heard of it."

As the monks discussed this mystery two women passed by. One was driving a cow home for milking, the other was moaning about her lost cow.

"Have you seen her?" the second woman asked the first.

"Oh yes," replied the first woman. "I saw her wandering down to Dunholm a few minutes ago."

When they heard this the monks leapt to their feet and joined the two women. "Can you show us the way to Dunholm?" asked their leader.

"Of course," said the woman who had lost her cow. "I'm going to find my animal there. Follow me."

Amazingly, the minute the monks now urged the horses to start pulling the cart again, it moved as if the wheels had been newly cleaned and greased.

The party moved off and soon came to a beautiful place. Steep, grassy, tree-lined banks led down into a valley where a river curled round in a great loop.

"What a wonderful place," said one of the monks.

"God had chosen Cuthbert's grave well," murmured another.

"There she is!" cried the woman suddenly. The red cow stood on a grassy ledge overlooking the river.

When the monks reached the spot where the cow was they knelt in prayer. Then they lifted Cuthbert's coffin off the cart and buried it there. Once they had rested they set about getting some materials and they built a little church over the spot where Cuthbert was buried.

For some years the simple church stood there. Then it was pulled down and a better one was built on the same spot. This happened again and again until a magnificent cathedral had grown from the first tiny church. It still stands there, in Durham, overlooking the River Wear, and inside still is the shrine of St Cuthbert.

Notes

Follow up themes: small beginnings; messages; faith.

Those familiar with Durham will appreciate the magnificent site on which the cathedral stands, dominating the city and the river below.

This story, with its tale of the dedicated monks, might be well suited to a prayer written by another saint. The prayer of St. Ignatius has been adapted as follows:

Let us learn to:
Give and not count the cost,
Work and not look for rest
Or always think about what is the reward.

55
Time to change

Augustine thought he had everything to make him happy – but did he?

"Where's the party tonight?"
"I don't know, but it's sure to be a good one."
"I know and I can tell you this, there's going to be the biggest spread of food there that you've ever seen."
"Well, in that case, I'm going to put my new clothes on."
"More new clothes, haven't you got enough?"
"I've never got enough."
The young men talking were Romans. They were all sons of rich Roman officers and lived in North Africa. All they thought about was enjoying themselves, how much money they could spend, and where the next party was. The most selfish of them all was a young man called Augustine.
Apart from being selfish and spoilt, Augustine was also clever. His job was teaching other young men how to speak well when they had to give speeches. One day a senior Roman officer sent for him.
"Augustine," said the man, "I've got good news for you. You're going to be given a new job in the great city of Milan."
"Fantastic," replied Augustine enthusiastically. He wasn't bothered about the new job but he'd heard all about the pleasures of Milan. "Now I'll really enjoy myself!" he thought.

So Augustine arrived in Milan, and things did not work out quite as he expected. He found that he was not being successful with his new pupils, and it worried him.

"I know what you can do," said one of his new friends. "Go and listen to the best speaker there is in the city – and see how he does it."

"Who's that?" asked Augustine.

"His name is Bishop Ambrose," replied the friend. "He's one of these Christian people – but don't listen to what he says – just how he says it."

So Augustine went to listen to Bishop Ambrose. He noted how the Bishop used his voice to get people's attention. First he spoke loudly, then softly; sometimes he was quick in what he said, at other times slow, soft and gentle.

At first Augustine took his friend's advice and concentrated only on how the Bishop spoke, but gradually as time went on Augustine found himself listening to what Bishop Ambrose was saying. Time passed and Augustine found himself going to more and more talks by this man. Now he had no interest in anything other than what the Bishop was saying. Eventually he stayed behind one day.

"Sir," he said to the Bishop, "may I talk with you?"

"Certainly," replied Bishop Ambrose. "I have seen you listening to me many times. I'm delighted to meet you."

So the two men talked, and became friends. They made an unlikely pair – the rich, reckless young Roman and the thoughtful Christian. Soon Augustine began meeting more Christians and gradually he began to realise that his way of life had not really made him happy at all. He had never even given a thought to other people – so it was time he started to do so.

"I'm going to be a Christian," he told his mother the same day.

So Augustine began to use his brains and energy in another way. He became a priest, and a very good one. He tried to help as many people as he could and he wrote books giving advice. Many people, seeing how wise he was, came to him with their problems and he spent hours talking with them.

It was not long before Augustine became a famous bishop himself.

Notes

Follow up themes: happiness; wisdom; hearing.

Augustine became Bishop of Hippo in Algeria (now called Bone). His most famous book was *Confessions* which was saved from Rome when the city was destroyed.

The following prayer could be used with this assembly:
Dear God, Help us to make our homes and schools better places, so that our towns and villages become better places, and our countries become better places and the world becomes a better place.

Teach us to be thoughtful and caring and not to put too much importance on those two words – 'I want'.

56
The wolf of Gubbio

How can we stop people behaving badly? This story of St Francis and the wolf suggests some thoughts.

"It has got to be killed."
"There's no other way. The sooner we do it the better."
A group of men armed with spears and bows and arrows stood talking just inside the walls of the Italian city of Gubbio. They were preparing to go out in search of a wolf which had been killing people and animals outside the city walls. Things had got so bad that crops lay unharvested because no-one dared go out to collect them in.
"Right – are we ready?"
"Yes, let's go. Open the gates."
"No – wait."
A man came hurrying up to the group, holding his hand out to make them pause. Immediately the men stopped. This was the famous Francis, a man known throughout Italy for his wonderful ways with animals and birds. Perhaps he had something important to say.
"Wait, my friends," said Francis. "I know this wolf has done you terrible harm but there may be another solution to the problem rather

than killing him."

The men looked doubtful. Francis went on. "I will go outside the walls first. If I meet the wolf I may be able to put things right."

"But … he'll kill you."

"Well, let me try first."

So the hunters reluctantly agreed, the great city gates were opened and Francis, unarmed, stepped out into the bare countryside. Behind him people crowded onto the city walls to see what would happen. Slowly he began to walk along the dusty trail away from the gates.

Meanwhile, lurking in a bush which overlooked the trail, the huge, shaggy wolf which was the cause of all the trouble lay motionless and watchful. He was starving as usual but couldn't understand why a man alone had left the city. Usually they came in groups these days, and always carried things which the wolf knew could hurt him. He watched … and waited.

Slowly the man came further and further from the city. No-one followed him and he carried nothing in his arms. Now … it was time to attack!

Francis saw the huge, bounding, snarling creature racing towards him as he neared a clump of trees. A great gasp went up from the watchers on the walls – surely Francis must now die.

The gap between man and wolf narrowed. Francis stood quite still and, as the wolf got even nearer, he raised his hand and made the sign of the cross. For a moment the wolf seemed confused. It stopped its threatening headlong dash, slowed and then crouched, still on the ground.

Francis moved slowly towards it, talking all the time in a soft voice as if it were another human.

"Calm down, calm down. You have done terrible things for which you should be punished but, I know you have only done them because you were starving and desperate."

By now the man had reached the cowering creature and, to the astonishment of the people watching, he put out a hand and began stroking its head.

"Now, we're going to put this right," went on Francis. "You and I are going to go back to the city and I'm going to ask the people there to feed you and see that you are never starving again. For your part – you will never hurt any living creature again."

At this the wolf slowly raised its paw, and Francis took it in his hand. Then getting to his feet he set off back to the city with the wolf loping behind him as if it were a trained dog. From that moment on the wolf lived at peace with the people of Gubbio.

Notes

Follow up themes: animals; solutions; behaviour.

A useful address is connection with this story could be: RSPCA, Causeway, Horsham, West Sussex RH12 1HG.

An appropriate Bible reference could be:

Let us never tire of doing good, for if we do not slacken our efforts we shall in due time reap our harvest. Therefore, as opportunity offers, let us work for the good of all." *(Galatians 6: 9-10)*

(This passage could be used as a concluding prayer.)

57
That's what we'll do

Sometimes making decisions is not easy and to make the right ones we may need help. This morning's story is about a very important decision.

"What do I need most of all to be a good king? How can I get my people to respect me?"

These were the sort of questions which filled the mind of the young king. He wanted to be fair and wise in his judgements so he spent long nights praying that he might be given the wisdom to rule well. The young king's name was Solomon and his wisdom was soon to be tested.

"What is that disturbance out there?" asked Solomon one day as he heard screaming and shouting outside his palace.

"I'll find out at once, your majesty," said one of his ministers, as he hurried out.

The minister came back very quickly, looking worried.

"There are two women out there, sir. Both insist on seeing you, but I'm not sure I would advise it."

"Why is that?"

"Well it seems an impossible situation. They have with them a baby and each insists that the baby belongs to them."

"Tell the guards to bring them in," ordered the king.

"Yes majesty," answered the minister reluctantly.

A few minutes later two women stood before the king. Both were angry and hot and distressed. One of them held a baby in her arms.

"Now," said Solomon in a calm voice, "I'm going to give each of you the chance to tell me your story – and then I'll make my judgement."

As soon as the king had finished speaking one of the women burst out excitedly.

"It's my baby, it's my baby," she said. "He was asleep and during the night this woman exchanged him for her baby who had died."

"That's not true," burst out the other woman. "That's not true at all!"

The king held up his hand. "Please," he said, "this is a very sad story indeed, and although the baby can only belong to one of you the best way to solve this problem is to …"

The king paused and beckoned over a guard as the two tearful women waited.

"Take out your sword," Solomon ordered the guard.

As the guard reached for his sword everyone around held their breath.

"Now," went on the king, "I want you to cut the child in two so that these two women can have half of the child each."

A terrible cry burst from one of the women and she threw herself on her knees before the king. "No your majesty, no, please don't kill him. Give him to her – but please don't kill him."

The king put his hand on the distraught woman's shoulder. "Now," he said, "we know who the real mother of this child is."

Notes

Follow up themes: families; being fair; justice; decisions.

The source for this very well known Bible story is 1 Kings 3: 16–28.

Some follow up work might be done on the difficult decisions people in important positions often have to make.

A useful Bible reference in connection with this is:
When a man has been given much, much will be expected of him; and the more a man has entrusted to him the more he will be required to pay. *Luke 12: 48*

Concluding prayer:
Let us pray that if we have a decision to make we are given the wisdom to do it well, and that we are at all times honest and truthful in all our dealings with other people. Amen.

58
Keep on trying

This morning's story is about a young man who, through no fault of his own, was unpopular. How he overcame his difficulties make an impressive story in determination.

The Bishop was speaking to some other priests.

"We need a priest for the parish of Holy Trinity Church in Cambridge," he said. "Charles Simeon is one of our best young men so he is going to get the post."

When Charles heard this he was very pleased. He had always been a good athlete and had worked very hard to make himself a good scholar. He had always wanted to be a vicar and was a kind and thoughtful man. But he had a great shock when he got to Holy Trinity.

"Have you heard about this new man we're getting?" people were saying.

"Yes – and we don't want him. We all want John back here as the vicar. He was the best curate we ever had."

"Well, how can we get rid of this new man then?"

"We'll make his life as miserable as we can – that's how."

So when Charles arrived he found everybody unfriendly and unhelpful. Nobody would speak to him and dreadful things happened. These were the days when the people who went to church often owned the pews they sat in. Well, the people of Holy Trinity were so keen to get rid of Charles that they stayed away from church, and locked their pews so that nobody else could use them.

"Hmm, this is a bit of a problem," thought Charles. "However, if I get some other seats put in the church then people who want to come can sit on these."

So Charles organised some new seats for the church but on the first Sunday after they had been put in he got another shock when he arrived to take a service. The churchwardens were very busy throwing all the new seats out into the churchyard!

Charles kept on trying but it was still very difficult. Another trick the churchwardens used was that before an evening service they would lock the church doors so that people coming to the service were left standing out in the street.

As you know however a vicar doesn't just preach in church. He goes round the homes in his parish speaking to those who are ill, encouraging those who need help and advising those who are worried. Charles did all of these things really well and many people came to know him as a generous man who would always do all he could to help others.

Other conversations began to take place in the parish.

"Isn't it time we did something about those people who are making life difficult for the vicar in his church?"

"Yes, especially when so many of us want to go to church."

"Perhaps we ought to go and see these churchwardens and sort things out."

So there was another great meeting and all those who had not wanted Charles as Vicar began to think again.

"Perhaps we've been too hasty," they said. "He seems to be doing a very good job in the parish. I vote we try and help him for a change."

So everything started to change. The church of Holy Trinity became packed on a Sunday and people listened, repeated and thought about what Charles had to say. And he kept on saying it, and trying to do good, for year after year after year. The amazing thing was that after such a dreadful start Charles stayed as the vicar of this church for over fifty years. His determination and great qualities as a man eventually made him admired by everybody.

Notes

Follow up themes: being fair; popularity/unpopularity; qualities.

Charles Simeon was born in Reading in 1759 and died in 1836. His name is still familiar in ecclesiastical circles because he founded the Simeon Trustees who sought to acquire church patronage.

The prayer for this morning could be:
Let us think this morning about difficulties. Let us remember that there are difficulties and disappointments in everyone's life but it is how we deal with them which is important. Let us pray that we might be given strength, courage and determination when we are faced with problems in our own lives. Amen.

59
Today not tomorrow

Don't boast about what you're going to do tomorrow; you don't even know what will happen today. Proverbs 27:1.

Herbert looked down over the smoky chimneys and the narrow streets of the town below him. He stood high on a hill and the breeze blew through his hair and tugged at the sleeves of his jacket. Herbert was rich, but like most rich men, he wanted to be richer.

"And I know how I'm going to be," he thought to himself. "There are twenty houses down there that belong to me – and I'm going to raise the rent on all of them. Then with the extra money I get I'm going to build the best house in the country up here. I'll get the best architect to design it and the best builder to build it – everybody for miles around will know its mine."

Now the ordinary people who rented the houses Herbert owned didn't have much money, and they weren't very happy when the rents went up, especially as Herbert made no effort to improve the poor conditions of their houses.

However there was nothing they could do about it and with the extra money coming in, added to the large amounts he already had, work on Herbert's house soon began.

"Coming on nicely," remarked Herbert to the builder when the shell of the house was complete. "Now remember I only want the very best fittings used in every room, and make sure it's the finest wood for the doors and cupboards."

Several more weeks went by and one Wednesday evening Herbert stood again on the hill top. Behind him was his finished house, splendid in every detail. For weeks Herbert had been boasting to anybody who would listen, and most who didn't want to, about how much this had cost, and how good this was, and how great it would be to live here, and so on and on.

"Just think," he muttered to himself, rubbing his hands, "tomorrow I'm moving in. Tomorrow I'll be living in the best house around. I bet there's lots of people down there who would like to be me."

That night Herbert died in his sleep.

(*Based on the Bible story of the new barn – Luke 12, 16 – 20*)

Notes

Follow up themes: boastfulness; living for today; exploiting others.

Concluding prayer:
Dear God, Teach us the value of modesty. Help us to avoid boasting about all things we are going to do. Help us to live happily and contentedly each day as it comes, and to be thankful for it. Amen.

60
Let's celebrate!

'A merry heart keeps a man alive, and joy lengthens the span of his days.'
(*Ecclesiasticus 30:22*). *This story reminds us that opportunities to celebrate should be taken and enjoyed.*

King David had decided that there should be a great celebration.
"It's a great moment for us now that we Israelites have settled in the city of Jerusalem," he said. "Our people crossed a great desert, and Abraham once walked on this hill. This will be our holy city."

"Are we going to do something special to mark this moment, your majesty?" asked one of the King's ministers.

"We certainly are," replied the king enthusiastically. "We are going to bring the Ark of the Covenant in through the city gates, and then we're going to have a great celebration."

The Ark of the Covenant was a wooden box which contained the Ten Commandments. It was usually carried on poles by priests and was a sign of God's presence with his people.

Now the Ark was the Israelites' most precious possession and it was being kept in a barn some distance from the city. As part of the festival preparations a party of men went to the barn, put the Ark on a cart and attached the cart to some oxen. Then a group of priests walked before the cart as it began the journey to the city.

Hundreds of people joined the procession towards the city and thousands more waited for it to arrive there. When the two groups sighted each other a great roar of clapping and cheering filled the air. As the Ark came through the gates trumpets blew, cymbals clanged and the cheering reached new levels.

At the head of the procession King David danced and cheered as loudly as anybody. Finally the Ark reached the huge tent which had been set up to receive it. A huge feast was set up in and around the tent and again the king could be seen everywhere handing round food and laughing with pleasure.

At last the great day's celebrations were over and a tired, but happy King David returned to his palace. There he met a young princess who was called Michal. She looked very serious and disapproving.

"What's the matter, Michal?" asked the tired king. "You don't look very happy."

"It's ... well ... it's you," began Michal hesitantly. "You ... a king, dancing and handing round food. Kings shouldn't ... well, kings shouldn't do things like that."

For a moment David stood quite still. Then he took the young princess' hand.

"Today has been one of the greatest moments in our people's history," he said. "At last we are home in our holy city of Jerusalem, our terrible days in the wilderness of the desert are behind us. Today therefore was a moment to celebrate as the Ark was brought home. God doesn't want his people to be miserable but to enjoy our, and his, great moments."

Notes

Follow up themes: celebrations; family occasions.

Another useful Biblical quotation is: I know there is nothing good for man except to be happy and live the best life he can while he is alive. Moreover, that a man should eat, drink and enjoy himself, in return for all his labours, is a gift of God. *Ecclesiasticus 3: 12-14*

Concluding prayer:

Let us give thanks this morning for celebrations – these times of joy and excitement which we all enjoy. Let us pray too for those people who have little to celebrate and find it difficult to do so. Let us give thanks too for our families and friends who bring so much joy into our lives. Amen.

61
My house is ready

This story is a modern adaptation of the famous Bible story of building on firm foundations.

"Well, I want my place ready for the beginning of summer," said James positively.

"Yes, but ..."

"There's no 'buts' about it," went on James, dismissing Winston's interruption.

So the bulldozers and the builders arrived at the site where James' house was to be built. No sooner had the bulldozers scraped out some shallow foundations than the builders began to lay the bricks and set in the window and door frames. Every day the magnificent house went up quicker, and soon it was time for the beds and settees to be put in and the kitchen fitted out. In no time at all the place was finished, gleaming in the summer sunlight and full of lovely furniture and fittings.

"Well – how about that!" exclaimed James to Winston, the weekend after the work was done.

"It looks good, very good indeed," admitted Winston, "but ..."

"Oh you're a terrible man for 'buts'," said James, slapping Winston on the back. "Tell me, how's your house getting on?"

"Well," replied Winston, "we spent ages finding a site where the ground is really solid and then I asked the builders to dig very deep foundations to make sure everything would be really secure."

"Yes – but how long before your house is going to be up?"

"I think it will still be some time yet."

"There you are then – mine is already built and I'm enjoying this lovely summer weather living in it."

The months passed by. James had lots of parties in his house during the summer, whilst Winston watched his house growing very slowly indeed. Eventually it was nearly Christmas and the weather turned very bad indeed.

Gale force winds tore across the countryside and huge torrents of rain lashed down. Inside his newly finished house Winston looked round at the still bare rooms and was glad he was safe and sound inside. Outside the wind roared and the rain thundered on the roof. Suddenly Winston heard another sound – somebody knocking loudly on his front door.

"Come quickly!" said the man standing there when Winston opened the door. "We've got to help ... that new house belonging to James up the road – it's fallen down!"

"What!" gasped Winston. "What happened?"

"It was built far too quickly," shouted the man. "They built it on sandy ground and no really proper foundations were laid. Come on, let's go and help them get out of the wreck!"

Notes

Follow up themes: good foundations; taking care.

This famous Biblical story is recounted in the following passage:
"He is like a man who had the sense to build his house on rock. The rain came down, the floods rose, the winds blew, and beat upon the house; but it did not fall, because its foundations were on rock. But what of a man who hears these words of mine and does not act upon them? He is like a man who was foolish enough to build his house on sand. The rain came down, the floods rose, the wind blew, and beat upon the house; down it fell with a great crash." (*Matthew 7 : 24-27.*)

Concluding prayer:
Dear God, Help us to remember that we need firm foundations for whatever we do in our lives. Help us to build these foundations by working hard at school and also enjoying the friendships we make here. Amen.

62
A clever mother

The story of Moses' birth is one which shows the courage and ingenuity of a mother.

The Pharaoh strode up and down in the great room of his palace.

"These Hebrews," he called out to his listening ministers. "They make good slaves – but if there get to be too many of them they'll cause us trouble. So – from now on any Hebrew boys born must be thrown into the river."

The Egyptian soldiers set about carrying out this terrible order. Hebrew mothers took desperate measures to try and hide their babies. One of them was a woman called Jochebed and she had just had a son whose name was Moses.

"We've hidden this baby for three months," Jochebed said to her daughter Miriam, "but he's getting too big to hide any more. However I've got another plan ..."

Jochebed told Miriam her secret plan. Next day mother and daughter took the baby boy down to the river. There they floated him in a basket of reeds and pitch, near a part of the river where the king's daughter came to bathe.

Now the king's daughter felt terrible about this awful killing of Hebrew baby boys and when she saw Moses floating in his basket her first thought was that she should help this child.

"Go and get that Hebrew baby at once," she said to one of her servants, and at that moment Miriam, Moses' sister, stepped out from the bushes.

"Your highness," she said, bowing low, "If you intend to keep that baby shall I ask one of the Hebrew women to be his nurse for you?"

"That's a good idea," said the princess as the servant dragged the basket inshore. "As soon as possible if you please."

Hurriedly Miriam returned to her mother.

"It worked!" she gasped. "Your plan worked. Moses is safe and I'm going to take you to the princess so that you can be the nurse for the baby."

Jochebed smiled. "My baby will be safe," she said. "That's

wonderful – and what's more I'll be with him every day to look after him."

Notes

Follow up themes: mothers; surviving; great leaders.

Moses, whose father was Amram, had a brother Aaron as well as a sister Miriam. He was a great statesman, leader and folk hero. References to this story can be found in Exodus, which goes on to relate more of his great deeds.

Concluding prayer:

Let us give thanks this morning for all those people of courage and cleverness whose stories are such an inspiration to us. Let us also pray for those people today whose lives are worrying and difficult because of wars and cruel deeds. Amen.

63
Broken promises

The Pharaoh kept breaking his promises to let the Israelites leave Egypt – as a result his people suffered even more.

Moses and his brother Aaron were waiting to see the Pharaoh. Although Moses was the leader of his people his brother was much better at speaking, so he was going to ask again if the Israelites could leave Egypt.

A few minutes later the Pharaoh listened as Aaron spoke.

"Sir," said Aaron, "you have already seen what dreadful things have happened to your people because you won't let us Israelites leave Egypt."

"Hmm," said the Pharaoh, thinking about all those dreadful plagues of frogs and lice and boils. He had promised to let the Israelites go –

but then when things had calmed down again he had changed his mind.

"I must warn you again," went on Aaron, "unless you let us go the worst storm ever seen will take place."

"Hmm," said the Pharaoh, and Moses and Aaron again left in despair.

Now the Egyptian people had learnt that the terrible things the Israelites told them to expect did happen, so when rumours of the coming great storm got around there was panic everywhere. Workers left their fields, cattle were crowded under cover and everything came to a standstill.

Then the storm arrived with all its terrifying violence. Lightning seared across the sky, torrents of water crashed into the fields causing floods, and thunder roared continuously. Some Egyptians were killed and even the Pharaoh was terrified. He sent for Moses and Aaron.

"Stop it!" he cried. "Stop this storm. Your people can leave as soon as it stops!"

"Do you really mean it this time?" asked Aaron.

"I do , I do!" yelled the Pharaoh. "Now go and stop it!"

Moses and Aaron left quietly, and prayed that the storm would stop.

Within a day it had done so. Peace came back to the land as the drying sun shone down. Workers re-appeared in the fields and the cattle came out from under cover.

The Pharaoh looked out from his palace and smiled to himself.

"Well," he thought, "that's another threat out of the way. If those Israelites think I'm going to let them go now they're very much mistaken. In fact a little punishment wouldn't do them any harm – instead of being slaves just making bricks, they can now gather the straw to make the clay bricks stronger as well."

Little did the Pharaoh know that by breaking yet another promise he was going to make things much much worse for his people.

Notes

Follow up themes: promises; responsibilities; leadership.

The story of the ten plagues and the subsequent flight from Egypt can be found in the Book of Exodus. Exodus 9 is the source for this particular part of the story.

Should it be convenient to do so, this story could be linked with St Swithin's Day on July 15. Swithin died in 862AD and asked to be buried in a simple grave outside Winchester Cathedral. When the cathedral was rebuilt during the reign of William the Conqueror it was decided that such a famous saint should be reburied inside the cathedral and given a prominent tomb.

Work on the reburial began on July 15th 1077 – to be greeted immediately with torrential rain. The rain persisted for 40 days – thus convincing those concerned that Swithin did not want his grave moved.

Concluding prayer:

Let us think this morning about promises. A broken promise often results in someone being hurt or disappointed. Let us remember how we feel when we have been let down by someone else. Let us pray that we can always do what we promise. Amen.

IV

Stories from other religions and cultures

64
The lute

This story reminds us that our characters are made up of a combination of things – how we look, think, feel, behave etc.

The king was in his garden one night. It was warm, and the scent from the frangipani hung heavily in the air. In the sky above the garden a heavy melon of a moon hung over the trees.

"Ah," thought the king. "What a beautiful place this is. What more could I wish for?"

It was then that he heard a lovely sound in the distance. It soothed the king even more and gave him enormous pleasure. Then, as suddenly as it had started, it stopped. But – the king wanted more.

"Servant!" he cried and clapped his hands sharply.

Within a second a servant stood bowing before him. "Majesty?"

"That sound – did you hear it? I want it brought to me."

"But your majesty … I didn't … what …"

Just then, as if to save the servant from embarrassment, the smooth musical sound started again.

"There – now you hear it?" queried the king. "Find that sound and bring it to me."

"Yes Majesty." The servant bowed low, turned and left the garden.

About an hour later the garden was still bathed in moonlight, the scent of the flowers still hung in the air, but the king was getting impatient. "Why hasn't that sound arrived yet?" he thought irritably.

Just at that moment the servant re-entered the garden. He was carrying something with him.

"Well," asked the king sharply, "have you brought it?"

"Yes, your majesty," replied the servant, showing the king what he carried. It was a lute.

"That's not the sound," snapped the king. "I asked you to bring me the sound – that's just some piece of wood and … strings!"

"But the sound comes from this," explained the servant carefully.

"Where? When? How?"

"Well … it comes from all the pieces of the thing, your majesty. It's got to have wood here and a hole here and strings here."

"But which piece is the sound?"

"It ..." the servant began, but the impatient king snatched the lute from his hands. Then he started to take it to pieces – looking for 'the sound'. Do you think that he found it?

(Adapted from a Buddhist story.)

Notes

Follow up themes: the 'whole' person; tolerance; understanding.

Gautaina Buddha taught that 'I' was made up of five parts – the body, feelings, perceptions, intentions of the mind and consciousness. A 'being' is a combination of these mental and physical parts which are known in the Sanskrit as the *skandhas*. The story is an illustration of this concept.

This service could use a quotation from the Dhammapada (Buddhist Scripture) as the concluding prayer:

Conquer anger by love,
Evil by good.
Conquer the miser
With liberality,
And the liar
With truth.

65
Sweetening the message

This story is about a message which was given in a sign.

"Land – at last!"

The weary travellers gasped the words aloud as they dragged their small boats up onto the beach. It had been a long and dangerous journey but they had now reached the safety of land again. The sun beat down fiercely on the travellers and, once they had secured the boats, they sat on the sandy beach to discuss their future.

"Well, we've escaped from Persia," exalted one.

"Yes, but will we be allowed to stay here?" wondered another. "After all, they didn't like us practising our religion in Persia. Why should things be different here?"

"Oh I don't know," went on a third, "I've heard of the king here. His name is Rana and he is supposed to be a man of great wisdom."

"Look – there's somebody coming..."

The Persians on the beach looked towards the line of trees behind them and saw three men approaching. They were moving very slowly and the one in the middle was carrying something. Within a few minutes they had reached the newly arrived group. Two of them bowed politely and the third one spoke.

"This is a message for your leader," he said, and held out the bowl of milk he was carrying. It was full to the brim.

"It's a welcoming gift," exclaimed one of the Persians excitedly, "they're making us welcome!"

"Quiet," ordered the Persian leader, Omar. "Didn't you hear what the man said – it's a message not a gift."

Then, for several minutes, Omar gazed at the full bowl of milk. When he spoke again it was in a calm voice.

"Yes," he said. "I understand the message. The bowl of milk filled to the brim means that your land is already full of people – and we are not welcome here."

There were groans from the other Persians and the messenger carrying the bowl nodded his head to show that the message had been understood.

"However," went on Omar, "I have a message of my own I would like you to take back to King Rana. Wait here."

Having said this the Persian leader walked to the pile of supplies his people had brought with them. Returning with a packet of sugar in his hand he carefully tipped this into the bowl of milk and waited a few minutes for it to dissolve.

"Now, take this back to your master," he said.

As cautiously as they had come the three men disappeared back beyond the trees. Half an hour later Rana received them. He listened to what they had to say, and then tasted the sweetened milk. He smiled.

"Truly our visitors are led by a wise man," he said, "and I

understand his message. He has improved the milk with sugar and if we let his group stay they will improve our land by mixing with our people and making this a better place for all to live. Messenger – return and bid our new friends welcome."

Notes

Follow up themes: visitors; welcome; wisdom; tolerance.

The religious group of travellers were from Persia (now Iran) and they had landed on the Indian coast at a place called Sanjan. They worshipped the god Zoroaster and became known in India as Parsees.

Parsees have very high moral standards, aiming to be just and fair in all things. They seek to be of service to other people and consider telling a lie a great evil.

The following quotations help to illustrate these features:

"May we be those who make life progressive and purposeful." (*Parsee prayer*)

"Whatever is taught to you deliver back to those who are worthy." (*Rule for Zoroastrian priests*)

One of the above quotations could be used as a closing prayer for this assembly.

66
The wife who would not give up

This is a story of determination. It is about a wife who was brave, resolute and quick thinking.

"Well, can we be married, Father?"

Princess Savitri looked at her father King Ashvapati longingly. Ashvapati smiled sadly at his beautiful daughter. She wanted to marry Satyavan, a fine, handsome young man who was the son of Senapati, once a king but now a blind old man.

Ashvapati liked Satyavan very much but he had just heard some terrible news. The wisest man in the kingdom had told him that Satyavan would be a wonderful husband – but he would die exactly one year after his marriage.

"Father ... please ..." Savitri interrupted her father's thoughts.

"My dear," began the king, and then he told her the whole story. For a minute Savitri was still and silent. Then she spoke.

"I still want to marry Satyavan, but please, promise me you will tell no-one of what the wise man has said."

Ashvapati and his wife pleaded with Savitri to think of the future, but she was very determined. In a short while she and Satyavan were married.

They were very very happy. Satyavan was a hard worker and very proud of his beautiful wife. Savitri was loving and cheerful and never let her husband see how worried she was about the dreadful secret she carried. Every single day she prayed to the goddess who had the same name as she did.

Time passed steadily and Savitri had to try desperately hard to hide her worries. As the first year of the marriage drew to a close she found an excuse to go everywhere with her husband. Finally it came to the last day of the year ...

"We need some more wood," said Satyavan, "I'm going into the forest to chop some."

"I'll come with you," replied Savitri quickly.

"Oh, there's no need," laughed Satyavan. But Savitri went anyway.

Satyavan started to chop the wood and then ... suddenly ... he dropped the axe, staggered a few paces, and fell to the ground ... dead.

Savitri rushed towards him, but Yama the god of death suddenly appeared between her and Satyavan's body.

"Be gone woman," he hissed, " he is mine now."

"Either return him to me, or take me too," pleaded Savitri.

"Ha," mocked Yama, "you can try to come with me but ..."

He laughed because he knew no mortal could go where he was going. But Savitri believed that a year of prayer had given her strength Yama didn't know about. They set off on the long, long journey, and eventually came to the edge of the Earth.

"This is it," smiled Yama. "Now we will pass into the Kingdom of the Sun and nobody can stand the heat of Surya the Sun God except me, because I am his son."

"We'll see," said Savitri bravely.

"Look," replied Yama, who secretly was beginning to admire her courage, "go back now and I'll give your father-in-law his sight back so he can look after you."

"If he is given his sight back the thing he will want to see most is his son," replied Savitri instantly.

Without another word Yama plunged into the Sun Kingdom. Savitri followed him and sure enough her prayers were protecting her because she passed the terrible heat of the Sun god without scorching to death.

"All right, all right," snapped Yama when he saw this. "Go back and I'll make Senapati a king again."

"What's the good of that?" Savitri replied. "If Satyavan is dead then there won't be an heir to the throne."

At this Yama lost his patience and swept on hurriedly to the Kingdom of Death. He was just about to go in when Savitri grabbed him tightly.

"Let go of me, woman," he snarled, unable to cross the threshold.

"Only if you'll make me the mother of sons," gasped Savitri.

"Of course, of course," Yama said hurriedly, thinking that at last he'd found the promise to get rid of this determined woman.

"Thank you, Lord," said Savitri softly, "but how can I be the mother of sons when I have no husband?"

For a moment there was silence and then Yama's great body began to rock and shake – with laughter. Leaning backwards he roared until tears ran down his face. Finally he spoke.

"Savitri," he said, "you are well named after the goddess of wisdom and you have more courage than any other mortal that I have ever met. Go home to your husband."

So Savitri returned to Earth and found Satyavan full of health. What's more her father-in-law could see again, and he had regained his kingdom.

Savitri and Satyavan then settled down to having a long happy life together and they had many children.

(Adapted from an Indian/Hindu story)

Notes

Follow up themes: determination; love; happiness; values.

Savitri was the Hindu goddess of wisdom and learning.

This service might be ended with the following comment:
Let us think this morning about wisdom and courage. To help us do this we might listen to some very old words: 'The tree of wisdom has fibres of forbearance, deep roots of steadfastness, flowers of virtue, branches of awareness.'
(The latter part of this reflection is a Buddhist saying.)

67
The monument

Muhammad cared especially for poor people – hence his advice to the rich man who wanted to build a monument.

"There's somebody to see you," said Abdulla to Muhammad one day. The great prophet was resting after a journey from Mecca, but he nodded and asked Abdulla to show in his visitor.

"My name is Yazeed," said the visitor, bowing to Muhammad. "I've come to ask your advice."

Now Muhammad could see from his clothes that Yazeed was obviously a wealthy man. "I'll be pleased to help if I can," he replied.

"Well," went on Yazeed, "my dear mother, Amina, died a few weeks ago and I want to build a great monument in memory of her. I want it to be so big and impressive that everybody will remember her when they look at it."

"How can I help then?" asked Muhammad again.

"Well ... what sort of a monument shall it be ... what are your ideas?"

"Do you really want the truth?" asked Muhammad.

"Of course," replied Yazeed.

"Forget about a monument then," went on Muhammad. "Find a place near where many people live, and dig there the finest well you can. Then wherever poor people come to draw water from the well they will be grateful and remember, and give thanks to your mother."

So Yazeed did as Muhammad suggested.

Notes

Follow up themes: useful gifts; money; water.

A very pertinent quotation to use in connection with this story, and to provoke discussion is: 'The beggar was given a horse. He did not want a horse, only a meal.' (*Old Japanese saying.*)

Concluding prayer:

Let us pray this morning that we can be given the wisdom to always act as sensibly and usefully as possible. We pray also that those less fortunate than ourselves are given as much help and hope as possible. Amen.

68
Good advice?

This is the story of how an honest man got his just reward.

"Not another new law!"

"Afraid so."

"This king of ours – he makes our life a misery."

"Yes – he can't leave things alone for five minutes."

The people of Katah were miserable. Every week their king had a new idea and changed laws and rules. All they wanted was to be left in peace for a while.

Meanwhile, in his palace, the king, who was restless and energetic, was pacing up and down the royal throne room. Standing nervously in front of him were the so-called wise men who were his advisers.

"Well," snapped the king, "this new idea of mine to change the market place – do you think it will work?"

Five of the six advisers shuffled their feet and glanced at each other. Then they all tried to speak at once …

"Of course, your majesty …"

"Brilliant idea."

"Only somebody as clever as yourself could have thought of such a brilliant plan."

"First class."

"Your people will be so grateful."

Now these five advisers were weak men and they were afraid of what the king would do to them if they didn't agree with his every idea. Idi, the sixth of the group was old and really wise.

"You, Idi," said the king. "You haven't answered my question."

"Your highness," replied the old man, "you are a man of many wonderful ideas … but the people are tired of constant changes. To move the market place would be something they would not like at all."

"So!" said the king harshly, "Once again you disagree with me – and all the other wise men."

At this the king swept angrily out of the throne room and went to the royal bedroom. There he lay down on the bed, and thought.

"Five of my wise men agree with everything I say. One disagrees as often as not ... and come to think of it my subjects don't seem particularly happy. Which of my advisers is telling me the truth?"

So the king decided to set a test for his advisers. He sent for the palace cook and told him that he must secretly make a special cake. This cake must look magnificent on the outside but be full of ingredients which made it taste really horrible.

A week later the cake was made and the king sent for his advisers.

"Friends," he said when they arrived, "today we are celebrating the months of help you have given me. Servants, give each of my ministers a slice of cake."

Eyeing the lovely looking cake greedily, the advisers could hardly wait to have a slice.

"So – eat up, and tell me what it's like," shouted the king, clapping his hands vigorously. Each of the wise men bit deeply into their slice of cake. As they chewed and swallowed they were shocked – it tasted absolutely terrible!

"Well?" queried the king, "well – what about it?"

"Oh ... marvellous your majesty," spluttered one.

"Delicious," mumbled a pale-faced second.

"Fantastic taste," gasped a third, wondering how he could possibly eat another mouthful of the vile cake.

"Your majesty," said Idi calmly. "This is the most disgusting cake I have ever tasted. I think your cook must be trying to poison you. Dismiss him immediately."

"No," replied the king. "I won't dismiss him because I told him exactly how to make the cake – and only you, Idi, had the courage to tell me what it really tasted like."

"Sir," said Idi bowing low.

"I want you to go out into my country and bring me back five more men as wise and honest as yourself to advise me from this day onwards."

As Idi bowed again the king turned scornfully to the other five advisers who were cringing with fear and shock.

"Guards!" shouted the king. "Take them away, I never want to see them in my kingdom again."

(Adapted from a Ghanaian folk tale)

Notes

Follow up themes: respect for authority; honesty; courage.

This story could lead on to some detailed discussion and thought on such issues as: different kinds of 'lies' – those for personal gain, 'white' lies which are told to protect people and encourage them in time of illness, stress, grief etc., tact, discretion, consideration and compassion.

Concluding prayer:

Dear God, Please help us in our dealings with other people. Help us to be honest but not cruel or tactless, to be caring but constructive. Please give us the wisdom to give good advice if we are asked for it. Amen.

69
The power of words

This story reminds us that it is never wise to underestimate people.

Sekhti made his living by gathering salt and pods and seeds in the countryside, and then bringing them into town to sell at the market. It was very hard work, and didn't pay very much, and he had only three donkeys to help him do the carrying.

One day Sekhti was returning to town with his three donkeys all heavily laden. Part of the route was along a narrow canal tow path. When he reached the path he saw a large embroidered sheet spread over the path. A large and mean looking man stood by the sheet.

"Your sheet is spread over the path," said Sekhti.

"I know, I know," replied Hemti, the mean looking man, "it's drying out so please don't trample over it."

"But there's no room to pass ..."

"Oh that's all right, just go through a bit of this cornfield."

"Well, I'm not sure ..."

"Go on, it'll be all right."

So Sekhti's donkeys made a short detour away from the path along the edge of the cornfield, and as they did so they nibbled a few ears of corn.

"Got you, got you!" shouted Hemti, when he saw this. "Your donkeys have eaten some of my corn – that means you have broken the law and I can claim all the donkeys and their loads as my own."

No sooner had he said this than he clapped his hands and some servants appeared. Instantly they seized Sekhti's donkeys and gave the poor trader a few punches as well.

"Justice," muttered Sekhti, through bleeding lips. "I will have justice for this."

"Ha!" mocked Hemti. "Who will listen to a stupid peasant like you? I am the High Steward of this land so everybody will take *my* word for what happened."

Hemti had of course planned the whole thing just to get the donkeys and goods.

So Sekhti went to the Hall of Judgement to seek justice. When the lords there heard that a peasant was to make a complaint they acted just as Hemti had said they would.

"We don't really want to listen to this peasant whining. We know what Hemti's like but we'll support him anyway. Just let this Sekhti say his piece and then we'll get rid of him."

So Sekhti was allowed to tell the story. As soon as he started to do so the lords were astonished by his beautiful voice and the brilliant way he used words to convince them. Rather than make a decision they reported the case to the Pharaoh, and the great man himself came to make judgement.

Again Sekhti spoke with honesty, passion and just the right words. When he had finished the Pharaoh spoke.

"I believe you, Sekhti," said Pharoah. "Nobody would have spoken like you did if he was lying. Hemti will be punished immediately and your donkeys and goods will be returned to you. Furthermore I need good men like you so you will take Hemti's place as steward of the canal."

Justice had been done.

(Adapted from an old Egyptian story)

Notes

Follow up themes: power; justice; speech; honesty.

Useful Bible references: When a poor man speaks to you, give him your attention. (*Ecclesiasticus 4:8*). The tongue – it is a small member but it can make huge claims. (*James 3:5*)

Concluding prayer:
Let us give thanks this morning for the power of speech. Let us also pray for people who are unjustly treated. May they be given the words to make others listen so that justice can be done.

70
The travellers' rest

This is a story of how words and music persuaded a man to change his evil way of life.

Nanak, the great leader of the Sikhs, and his friend Mardana were on one of their journeys round India.

"What is this town we are coming to ?" asked Mardana.

"It is called Tolumba," replied Nanak, "and it looks as though there is somebody waiting for us." As he spoke Nanak nodded towards a tall, kindly looking man who was standing outside a cool pleasant house. As they neared him the man spoke.

"Welcome to Tolumba, friends," he said. "I can see you have travelled far but you are welcome to stay in my house. Whether a man is a Hindu or a Muslim he is welcome here."

As he spoke these words the man, who went on to say his name was Sajjan, bent low in a bow of greetings. Before he did so however Nanak had seen his eyes, and from the expression of greed in them the wise traveller knew that the welcome was false.

"We are neither Hindu nor Muslim," said Nanak to Sajjan's invitation, "but we believe in one God. We thank you for your invitaion to stay the night."

Nanak had been quite right to be suspicious of Sajjan. His purpose in inviting travellers to stay with him was to rob them while they slept. In this way he had grown rich.

After Sajjan had provided supper for the two travellers Nanak spoke to Mardana. "My friend, please get out your instrument and we will play and sing for our host."

So Mardana got out his musical instrument, which was rather like a guitar, and Nanak began to sing. He sang of what he believed, of how men should care about each other, help each other, try to do acts of kindness.

The beautiful music and thoughtful words seemed to hang in the cool air like a message of hope. As Sajjan listened his eyes filled with tears and he was bitterly ashamed of the dreadful things he had done.

"Forgive me, my friends," he burst out when the music was finished, and then he told Nanak the whole story.

From that moment Sajjan became a changed man and really did provide a house where travellers of all kinds could rest and be safe.

Notes

Follow up themes: forgiveness; being a good neighbour.

There are many stories about Guru Nanak, the first leader of the Sikhs. He lived in India from 1469 to 1539 and as well as founding a new religion he left many writings which were collected in the *Guru Granth Sahib*, the Sikh's Holy Book.

This morning's prayer could be an adaptation of some words from the Guru Granth Sahib:

Do not try to search for God a long way away but try to understand that His Word is in the hearts of everybody.

71
The exchange

Sometimes a brave and determined man finds everything going against him. That is when he needs a little help.

Bilal tried to stop the groans forcing themselves past his lips. The sun blazed down from the sky and the hot desert sand scorched his back. His hands and feet were tied to stakes driven into the ground and a heavy rock pressed down on his chest. He had been undergoing this torture now for several days. He remembered how it had all started …

"Bilal!" His master's voice called out harshly.

"Yes, master?"

"I have heard that you have been listening to this troublemaker Muhammad – and that you have been going around saying there is only one God."

"Yes, master."

"Well as long as you are my slave you'll stop such nonsense. All right?"

"No, master."

"No, master! How dare you speak to me like that – you a slave!"

"I cannot give up what I believe, master."

"Indeed – well, we will have to do something to change your mind then. Servants … !"

And so that was how Bilal came to be tied up in the burning sun for day after day. Each morning his master ordered him to apologise and give up his belief. Each morning Bilal refused. Now he knew he was near to death.

Then, through the heat and pain, Bilal was aware of somebody else speaking to him. "My friend – who is doing this to you – and why?"

Through half closed eyes Bilal saw the blurred face of Abu Bakr leaning over him. Abu Bakr was a Muslim like himself, but a very rich merchant. Bilal gasped out his story.

Abu Bakr went straight to the tortured slave's master. "I've got a bargain for you," he said jovially. "That Muslim slave of yours out in the desert – he's just about finished, but I like him. I'll exchange one of my stronger slaves, who doesn't believe what Muhammad says, for that Bilal."

Bilal's master pretended to consider this. Secretly however he couldn't wait to make the exchange – to get rid of that trouble maker who was now a physical wreck and get a fit young slave in his place...

"Agreed," he said finally.

When Bilal was released he was handed over to Abu Bakr.

"I don't want you to be a slave," said Abu Bakr, "so I'm going to make you a free man. I've got a feeling you can be a great help to Muhammad and the rest of us Muslims."

So Bilal was freed and soon recovered his strength. Years later when the first mosque was built in Medina Muhammad asked Bilal if he would take the job of calling people to prayer.

Notes

Follow up themes: determination; what people believe.

Concluding prayer:

Let us pray this morning for the ability to try and understand everybody else's point of view. Let us pray that we always have time to listen to the opinions of others. Amen.

72
The flood

One of the most famous stories in the Bible is that of Noah's Ark, but people of other religions believe that there was once a terrible flood which covered the earth.

It was very early in the morning, and cool.

"What a pleasant time this is to walk," thought Manu, "before the fierce heat of the sun."

He was walking beside the sacred River Ganges. Eventually it began to get hotter and hotter. Manu stopped and knelt down. He decided he would say his morning prayers here, and cool his face with the sacred water of the river. Bending low he scooped up two handfuls of water. Then he got a surprise!

There, swimming in the pool of water in his hands, was the tiniest of fish he had ever seen. Before he could do anything about it he got a second surprise – the fish spoke to him!

"Save me Manu," it cried, "save me. If you throw me back I won't live five seconds before another fish eats me."

Manu was astonished. Not only had the fish spoken to him but it had done so using his name. This must be a very special fish indeed. Keeping his hands carefully cupped together he hurried home as fast as he could and put the fish safely in a jar of fresh water.

More surprises were in store for Manu. The next one came a few hours later when he looked at the fish – only to find that if had grown so much it filled the jar. Quickly he seized the jar and hurried to a nearby pond with it. No sooner had he put it in the pond however than it began to grow again.

"This is amazing," thought Manu and taking the fish from the pond he carried it to a lake which was not far away. No sooner had he put the fish in the lake than it began to grow and grow again.

By now the fish was huge and Manu thought it would have to go in the sea. So, taking it from the lake, and staggering under its weight as he carried it, he headed for the sea which was not far away.

"There," he cried as he put it into the sea, "you will be one of the biggest fish in the sea and nothing will harm you … but …"

"Yes," replied the fish, "go on."

"Well …" muttered Manu, "… who are you?"

"I am pleased that you have asked," answered the fish, "because I have a very great job for you. I am the god Vishnu who looks after all the world. Something terrible is going to happen soon. A great flood is going to cover everything and drown everything – unless you do something about it."

"But what can I do?" asked the startled Manu.

"You must build a boat and then you must collect a pair of every kind of animal living in the world and put them safely in the boat. Then I will tow the boat to a safe place when the storms come."

So Manu went about his task and events happened just as Vishnu said they would. But, because of the great boat, life on Earth was saved.

(Adapted from a Hindu legend)

Notes

Follow up themes: care of the environment; tolerance – different people's beliefs.

Some teachers may want to compare this with the story of Noah's Ark for which the Bible reference is Genesis, Chapter 2.

Concluding prayer:

Let us pray this morning for tolerance and respect for other people's views and beliefs. Let us remember an old saying which will help us to do this – 'always be friendly and you will travel the road of happiness.'

73
A Buddhist tale

Sometimes it is very painful to stand up for our beliefs – as the Buddhist monk in this story found.

"I'll be glad when I've got this job finished," muttered the jeweller to himself. As he spoke his fingers fluttered like butterflies over the gleaming pearls and string. He was making a necklace for the king.

"Last one," he thought, picking up the biggest and most beautiful pearl of all. Then, just as he was about to thread it, he saw the monk approaching his door.

"Come in, come in," called the jeweller. "Now if you'll just wait a minute I'll go and get you some rice from the kitchen."

The monk bowed his head in thanks and stood there in his saffron robes whilst the jeweller put down the last huge pearl and moved off to the kitchen. No sooner had he gone than a large goose came into the room, saw the pearl, thought it was food, and swallowed it.

The monk was aghast. The pearl was gone and when the jeweller returned he would certainly think the monk had taken it. At the same time if he told the jeweller what had happened then the goose might be killed. As the Buddha taught that every living thing was our brother, and he was a Buddhist monk, he couldn't allow this to happen.

The jeweller returned.

There was a long pause.

"Very well," said the jeweller slowly, putting down the bowl of rice. "I would not have expected someone like you to steal a pearl, but if you return it now we'll say no more about it."

The monk was in trouble. He couldn't tell the truth and he couldn't lie. Stuttering nervously he raised his hands as he pondered what to do and say. At this the jeweller became furious.

"I've given you a chance," he roared. "What sort of chance do you think the king will give me when he finds out that the biggest pearl of the necklace is missing? Well ... answer me. He'll kill me, that's what he'll do."

At this the jeweller lost his temper and began beating the monk. The monk took all the blows meekly but then, in the commotion, the goose got in the way of one of the jeweller's wild swings and was killed instantly.

At once the monk fell to his knees beside the dying goose, with tears streaming down his face.

"What's this?" cried the astonished jeweller. "You take my blows without a word, yet when a goose is killed you weep?"

"It is like this," said the monk, and he told the jeweller the whole story.

Without a word the jeweller took out a knife and cut open the goose's stomach. There lay the pearl.

At this the jeweller fell to his knees and took the monk's hand.

"Forgive me for doubting you," he said, "and forgive me too for killing this our brother. You have taught me today something of the Buddha's teaching and from now on I will try and live by his words of wisdom."

The monk, stiff and sore as he was, and sorry for the death of the goose, rejoiced. The jeweller had not only got back his pearl but he had learned something of the teaching of the Buddha.

Notes

Follow up themes: faith; courage; teachings of others.

Buddhists believe that following the Eightfold Path brings enlightenment and Nirvana – the end of all suffering. To follow the Eightfold Path one must have the right grasp of the Four Noble Truths which observe that: 'Suffering is to be found everywhere; it is caused by selfishness and self-interest; it is cured be ending demanding thoughts; this can be done by following the Eightfold Path.'

A useful 'prayer' to end this assembly could be another piece of Buddhist advice:

> If a man speaks or acts
> With an evil thought,
> Pain follows him.
> A tamed mind
> Brings happiness.

74
Reminders

We have diaries to remind us of what we are doing next week; calendars to remind us of birthdays. There are other kinds of reminders.

John was on holiday in a most unusual place – Tibet. When he was there he saw a group of people moving about one day.

"What are those people?" he asked his father.

"They're Buddhist monks," replied John's father.

"They look as if it's very uncomfortable for them to walk."

"Yes – you'll see why if you look at their boots."

So, trying not to be rude, John peered at the boots the monks were wearing. They looked awful and were a most peculiar shape. Just then, one of the monks saw John staring, and came across to him with a smile.

"I noticed you looking interested. Can I help?"

"Well," mumbled John, "I didn't mean to stare rudely … but …

your boots ... I mean ..."

"Ah," the monk's smile was now more knowing. Putting a foot out so that John could see the boot even more plainly he began to explain.

"Now, look at the toe of the boot. You'll see that it is curved up and looks like a pig's snout. It's supposed to, because the pig stands for confusion in the Buddhist religion. So this part of the boot is a reminder not to get confused by things."

"I see," said John, "but what about those bumps on the side?"

"These, you mean," went on the monk, running his finger over the lumpy sides of the shoe. "These remind us of a rooster, and that stands for being too attached to earthly things."

"And what about this curved shape which goes right from the top of the shoe to its tip?" asked John.

"Well, look at it carefully," smiled the monk. "What do you think it looks like?"

"Er ... well ... a snake," suggested John uncertainly.

"Exactly," cried the monk. "A snake it is, and the snake stands for hatred. So you see if we wear these boots, which I might tell you are not very comfortable, we keep looking down at them and seeing reminders of what we must always try to avoid in our lives."

Notes

Follow up themes: reminders; qualities; temptations.

Buddhists believe that suffering in the world is the result of dependence on the wrong things and that they must seek to 'not do any evil, cultivate good, purify one's mind.'

There is a refreshingly optimistic quotation from Zen Buddhist sayings which could be used to end this assembly:

Such is life
Seven times down
Eight times up.

75
Lost and found

Do we make the most of our time? Are we generous enough? Perhaps the twists and turns of this old story provide some answers.

The king was often sad – and when he was, his chief minister, in a very polite way of course, tried to persuade him to be more cheerful.

"I wonder how cheerful *he* would be if he was in real trouble?" thought the irritated king one day. He decided to find out.

"Ah," he said when the minister next appeared before him. "I want you to guard one of my most precious jewels for me for a week."

"Of course, your highness," replied the minister, who was rather flattered to be given such an honour.

"But of course if you lose it ..."

The king didn't need to finish this sentence!

So the minister was given an enormous ruby to look after. Taking it home he put it safely in a box. What he did not realise however was that the king had sent spies to follow him, and as soon as the minister left his house again they took the jewel from its hiding place and brought it back to the king.

"Now we'll see what happens," thought the king when he got the jewel back, and opening a window, hurled it into the nearby river. The next day he sent for the minister again.

"Thank you for looking after my ruby – please bring it back to me this afternoon."

"Certainly your majesty," replied the minister, but of course when he went to collect it, the ruby had gone. After searching his house from top to bottom he returned to the king.

"Sir ... I ... I'm afraid the ruby has been stolen."

"Stolen – stolen!" roared the king. "What sort of a trick is this? Unless that jewel is returned to me within three days, you – and your wife – will die."

Of course the minster knew he would never find the ruby in three days so he told his wife the dreadful news.

"We have no hope of finding the stone," he said, "and we are certain to be put to death. So, with only three days of our lives left we must live them as fully as we can."

So the minister's house became the liveliest and most brightly lit house in the city. Wonderful meals were prepared and beggars came and ate their fill. Presents were given to all their friends and shopkeepers and tradesmen were given extra gold coins for their service over the years. Hardly anyone in the town was overlooked or not rewarded.

"They are the kindest people I have ever known," said a poor flower seller to her friend, a fisherman's wife on the day before the couple were to die.

"I wonder if they'd like one of my husband's fish for a last meal tonight?" replied the fisherman's wife. "It's time somebody tried to return some of their kindness."

Some time later, complete with one of the biggest fish her husband had ever caught, the fisherman's wife presented herself at the minister's house. There, the minister's wife thanked her graciously and gave her two gold coins for her trouble and kindness.

"We're going to eat splendidly tonight," said the wife to her husband and then, taking a knife, she cut into the fish. At once the tip of the knife hit something hard – and the ruby fell out onto the plate.

The astonished and relieved minister could hardly wait to get the ruby back to the palace. The equally astonished king received the jewel very solemnly – and then told the minister the whole story.

"Of course I would not have had you killed," he said. "I just wanted to teach you a lesson – but I think we have all learned something from what has happened."

(*Adapted from an old Indian story dating from the nineteenth century.*)

Notes

Follow up themes: advice; time; giving and receiving.

Although this is an Indian story there is a quotation from the Talmud which is appropriate to it: 'A man will have to give account on Judgement Day of every good thing he could have enjoyed – and didn't.'

Concluding prayer:
Let us pray that despite the successes and disappointments of our lives we can stay the same and always behave cheerfully, kindly and generously to other people. Amen.

76
Worth waiting for

This is about how a very important person was aware of the importance of an 'ordinary' man.

Vijay was flustered. For days everybody had been saying, "The Buddha is coming, the Buddha is coming!" and like everybody else Vijay wanted to hear the Buddha's great words of wisdom. And now everything was going wrong!

"I'll never get there at all at this rate," muttered Vijay to himself. He'd just been about to set off when he'd noticed that his cow had broken loose and escaped. For a poor farmer like himself, the loss of a cow meant he wouldn't be able to make a living.

So Vijay set off into the forest to look for the cow. After searching for hours he found it and brought it back home. He was hot, tired and hungry but ...

"I haven't time to eat," he thought, "everybody will have eaten by now but if I hurry I might just be able to hear the last few words of what the Buddha has to say."

So once more Vijay hurried through the forest, this time to the huge clearing where he knew everyone was gathering to meet the Buddha. Even more tired, hot and hungry he eventually reached the crowded clearing – and got a surprise.

People were milling round but the Buddha was sitting calmly, silently waiting. When he saw Vijay his face widened into a smile and he said to some people nearby, "Please bring some of the food that's left for my friend Vijay."

Vijay was absolutely astonished for, of course, he had never met or even seen the Buddha. Gratefully he began to eat as quickly as he could. But he could hear lots of grumbles as he did so.

"What are we waiting for? Somebody can't get here promptly – so we have to wait! This is too bad!"

The Buddha heard these grumbles too, and as soon as Vijay had finished eating he stood up.

"My friends," he said, "I know more than you so I can tell you that Vijay has had more of a struggle than any of you to get here today. If

I had begun to talk while he was hungry and rushed – how well would he have been able to listen? But now that he is well fed and calm – so we will begin."

Then the Buddha began to speak and everything was forgotten as the crowd listened to his marvellous words.

Notes

Follow up themes: judging others too hurriedly; consideration; surmounting irritations.

In connection with the point of grumbling about others the Dhammapada (Buddhist Scripture) says : 'The fault of others is easily seen; our own is difficult to see.'

The concluding prayer for this assembly could be an adaptation of one of the Buddha's sayings:
Let us think this morning about caring. When a person really cares about others he lights up the world, just as the moon does when it escapes from behind a cloud.

77
The argument

Sometimes a small incident shows how foolish it is to argue – as this story shows.

It was burning hot, and Rajindra the farmer desperately needed water for his land. Bending in the stream he was disappointed to see that there was even less water than there had been the day before. Barely a trickle crept over the stony river bed.

"Hey, there's not enough water there for two of us – and that stream is on my land."

Rajindra glanced up at this harsh shout. Looking at him angrily from the other side of the stream was his neighbour Shavnarine.

"This stream is between our lands – and we've always shared it," protested Rajindra, equally angrily.

"Rubbish, and if that's the attitude you're going to take ..."

And so in the desperate heat and drought the two men forgot the work they had to do and spent several minutes shouting insults at each other. Finally both stormed off with threats of bringing others for a fight to see who could use the stream.

An hour later the banks of the stream were lined on either side with angry men. Sticks were being waved threateningly and the once peaceful valley was full of angry shouts and insults.

"We'll soon see who the river belongs to! Just you try coming over here – go on and try it! You'll never get a drop of this water after this!"

While the men were yelling like this a little boy who had been playing on one of the banks slipped and fell into the stream. One of the sharp stones cut his knee and he let out a cry of distress. At once a man from each side jumped in to help the boy. As they did so they saw a swirl of blood from the cut on his knee mingle with the water.

"If we go on like this there'll be more blood in this water," said one of the men.

"You're right," replied the other, "do we want that?"

Looking at the trickle of water, and then each other for a moment longer, the men suddenly reached out and shook hands. At once all the anger and selfishness went out of both groups and they were shaking hands and apologising for their selfishness and anger.

Shavnarine sought out Rajindra. "I'm sorry, neighbour. We've always shared this stream no matter how little water was in it. Let's carry on doing that."

"I agree," replied Rajindra, "now look, you take what you need first."

The next week rain came again to the valley and the stream was once again full to the brim with plenty of water for everybody.

(Adapted from an Indian folk tale)

Notes

Follow up themes: water; arguments; sharing.

There is a useful Biblical quotation to match this story. This can also be used as a short concluding prayer:

'If you answer people gently they won't get angry; but sharp words stir up anger.' *(Proverbs 15:1)*

The 'environmental aspect' of this story might provoke further follow up work and the following address could be useful in this context : Friends of the Earth, 377 City Road, London EC1.

78
The impostor

Sometimes we are tempted to pretend that we are more important than we really are. As this story shows, this is a mistake!

"There must be something here," thought the jackal as he turned the corner into the long empty street. The city's streets at night were one of his favourite hunting grounds. Picking up the scent of something good, he moved amongst the litter searching for it.

Suddenly there was a great commotion ahead of him. Racing round the corner came a pack of savage, wild dogs. They were also hunting for food and when they saw the jackal they immediately gave chase.

"I must hide somewhere," thought the jackal desperately as he fled. Then, out of the corner of his eye he saw some barrels standing beside a house. Immediately he leapt in one and the dogs careered past without knowing where he had gone.

Now the jackal couldn't have stayed in the barrel long because it was full almost to the brim with liquid. When the dogs had disappeared he climbed out, shook himself and went on his way.

When he got back to the jungle it was almost light and he saw a tiger coming towards him. Getting ready to run for his life again he was astonished when the tiger turned and ran off as if it were terrified. Amazingly enough whatever creature the jackal met bolted immediately.

By now the sun was high and the jackal looked down at himself. "Well I ..." he began. He now knew why the other animals had run off. From top to toe he was bright blue in colour!

"There must have been some dye in that barrel I hid in," he thought. "The other creatures have never seen an animal this colour and they're frightened. Now's my chance!"

The next time he saw an animal the jackal called, "Hare – I command you to stop at once!"

The terrified hare, fearing for its life, stopped. The jackal went on, "I am from the god Indra. I have come to rule this jungle. Tell all the animals except jackals that I want to see them here at sunrise tomorrow."

Well, when the message got round none of the animals wanted to offend this creature who had been sent by the gods. With the exception of the jackals they all arrived at sunrise the following morning.

"Now," said the jackal, "obey my orders and you will be quite safe."

Then he continued – the lion and tiger must bring him food, the antelope must carry his messages, the monkey had to keep him cool ... and so it went on. Within days the jackal was living like a king – comfortable, well fed and in command of all around him.

Then, a week or two later, a pack of jackals passed near his court. As they did so they howled loudly. The jackal was so pleased with himself that, before he could help himself, he let out a great howl in reply.

Unfortunately the tiger was bringing him some food at the time. No sooner did he hear the noise than he knew the animals had been tricked.

"This is no king," he snarled, "it is a jackal."

So saying he leapt upon the blue jackal and killed him.

(Adapted from the Panchatantra*)

Notes

Follow up themes: truth; modesty; deceit.

There is a useful Biblical quotation which is relevant to this story:
'Be humble always and gentle. Be forbearing with one another and be charitable.' (*Ephesians 4:2*)

Concluding prayer:
Let us try always to do the best we can in any situation, but let us not be tempted to think that we are more important than anyone else. Teach us hard to value and understand the meaning of modesty. Amen.

* *The Panchatantra* is a collection of Indian folk tales. They were originally supposed to have been told by a wise priest to three young Indian princes in order to give them guidance as to how to live their lives. Consequently they include a mixture of humour, strong moral points and a wide appreciation of life.

V

Christmas Stories

79
The visitor

Jesus' birth is a reminder not to judge people by appearances. Several people made that mistake in this story.

It was Christmas Eve and Ivan the Good, Czar of Russia, stroked his chin.

"I wonder how the poor people of my great country spend Christmas," he said, glaring at his rich and servile courtiers.

"Oh, very well I'm sure your Highness."

"Oh yes – you don't want to be concerning yourself about them my Lord. Certainly not, your majesty – it could be dangerous."

"Out of my way," snapped the Czar.

Hurrying to his room, he found the oldest, dirtiest clothes he could get. After putting them on he rubbed his hands and face with dirt, and set off.

Some hours later this 'beggar' was knocking at the door of a small house in a village. A man answered the knock.

"Sir," said the disguised Czar, "could you possibly let me stay with you for the night? I promise I will pay you later."

"You, pay me later! A likely story. Be off with you!"

So the Czar went on his way round the poor village. Some people just told him to clear off, others made all sorts of excuses, but nobody was prepared to give him a meal, or let him stay the night with them.

Finally the Czar reached the poorest, scruffiest looking house in the entire village. He raised his hand to knock on the door ... when it opened, creaking on ancient, unoiled hinges.

"Come in, come in," invited the tired looking man who had opened the door. "I've seen you going round the village and I noticed how everybody turned you away. Well, you're very welcome here, but I must warn you about certain things."

"Thank you for the invitation sir," answered Ivan, "but please ..."

The tired man went on. "Well, I've a very sick wife and six children. She is too ill to cook and I haven't time so all we have to eat is a loaf of bread – but you're welcome to share. There again, with so many bodies in the house we have no beds to spare but if you're happy to, you can sleep on straw on the floor like I do."

"You are most kind," said Ivan. "I'm very grateful for whatever you can let me have – and I will certainly repay you later."

"Oh don't give that a thought," went on the old man, "come in and make yourself as comfortable as possible."

So Ivan spent Christmas Eve in the poor man's house. Next morning he noticed that there were no Christmas presents for anybody, but the man was enormously kind to his children, and his sick wife tried desperately to be cheerful even though she was in pain.

When it was time to go the Czar shook the poor man's hand firmly. "Thank you again for your kindness," he said. "I'll be back to pay you shortly."

"Oh, I've told you not to worry about that. I'm sure you're poorer than we are – here look – take a bit of this bread with you to help you on your way."

With a nod and a smile Ivan left.

Three hours later the poor man was busy cleaning up the house as best he could when there was a thunderous knock on the door. Opening it nervously he was astonished to see the 'beggar' standing there again – but dressed magnificently in the robes of a king! Several people stood in a line behind this obviously important person.

"My friend, I've come to repay your kindness," smiled Ivan.

The poor man just stood there with his mouth open.

"First let me introduce myself properly," went on Ivan. "I am the Czar of all of Russia. Now, this person here is a doctor who has come to make your wife better; these people behind him have brought you some food and fuel and, at the end there is somebody who has a Christmas present for everybody."

"But ..." interrupted the poor man.

"Oh, I haven't finished," continued Ivan. "Tomorrow, when the holiday is over, I want you to come to the palace at 10 o'clock. I could do with an honest, kind man working for me. A job will be waiting for you."

Needless to say it was the best Christmas the poor man had ever had.

Notes

Follow up themes: appearances; Christmas; rich and poor; gratitude.

Concluding prayer:
Dear God, Help us to treat everyone in a way which we would like them to treat us. Help us to remember that one of the great pleasures of Christmas is giving as well as receiving. Help us to be the sort of person others would like to know. Amen.

80
Thardon's Christmas

Apart from the unfortunate traveller at the beginning of the story, everybody else gets what they deserve for this Christmas.

The branches reached threateningly across the moonlit sky and the wind howled mournfully through them. Crouched low over his horse's neck the lone rider drove his mount through the bitter night. There were two days to go to Christmas and …

"Whoa, whoa," yelled the rider urgently, reining back his sweating horse. There on the ground ahead lay a man and nearby his horse stood aimlessly. The lone rider, whose name was Will, leapt from the saddle and crouched by the man on the path.

"You've … you've got to help," whispered the injured man. "Highwaymen have shot me and taken all the money I had on me … but my horse galloped off in fright and has just returned and …"

"Steady, steady," said Will quietly, "I'll get help and …"

"No," snapped the injured man, with a great effort. "You don't understand. In the saddle bag there's enough gold to buy the Christmas food for the village of Thardon. I was sent to …"

The man's head dropped. He was dead.

Will knew that the village of Thardon was about ten miles away. He covered the dead man as best he could and then looked in the saddle bag. Sure enough a bag of gold clinked in his hands as he delved inside. Will was a poor man and …

"What's that got to do with it?" he thought to himself. Quickly he pocketed the gold and leading the stray horse behind his own he galloped as fast as possible to the nearby town of Fullbridge.

At Fullbridge Will sought out the mayor and told him the story. As a result some men were sent to bury the dead messenger, and Will bought all the Christmas provisions for Thardon. Packing these in two big containers he hung them across the spare horse's back and set off for Thardon.

He'd been travelling about an hour when he heard the hoof beats behind him. Turning, he saw in the pale moonlight the flapping cloaks and masked faces of the gang of highwaymen. Spurring his horses forward he began a desperate race for the village. Slowly but surely the outlaws closed in on him. Nearer and nearer .. and then Will saw a party of men galloping towards him!

As they swept by the highwaymen saw they were outnumbered and turned to flee. It was too late. Within minutes they had been rounded up and, with bound hands, were led into the village behind Will.

The leader of the group joined Will. "We came out to look for our messenger – but instead we caught those criminals. And – who might you be, young man?"

Will told him the whole story, and the man was quiet until they reached the village square where a large crowd had gathered. The leader of the riders shouted in a loud voice: "I've bad news friends. Our friend Joseph is dead!"

There was a groan from the crowd.

"But," went on the leader," we have caught those responsible and, thanks to the honesty, courage and effort of Will here, we've got our Christmas provisions."

A great cheer filled the night air and Will found his hand being shaken and his back being thumped.

"Well done! Thanks! You're a true friend. Joseph would have been proud of you."

And so Will felt that he had helped the people of Thardon to enjoy their Christmas. When it was all over, rather than continue on his wandering ways he decided he would like to stay there and, a few years later he was the very popular mayor of the village.

Notes

Follow up themes: travel; Christmas; honesty.

Concluding prayer:

Let us pray at Christmas time for those people who are tempted, greedy, bitter, selfish and unhappy. Let us pray that they can be shown that there is a better way to live and that honesty, kindness, friendship and care are waiting to be given and received. Amen.

81
The king
and the carvings

The value of things given often lies in the reasons why they were given – as this story shows.

King Boris was a man admired by everybody. He was kind, thoughtful, fair and did as much as he possibly could for the people he ruled. One of his subjects was an old woodsman whose hobby was carving.

"Nobody could have been more helpful than the king when this village was in trouble," thought Ivan the woodsman one day. "I wonder if he would accept one of my carvings as a gift for Christmas."

So Ivan got to work and, doing his very best, he carved a small bird. Then he went and stood on a woodland path which he knew the king rode along from time to time. Sure enough, after several hours the king appeared. He saw Ivan.

"You look as if you have been waiting there a long time, friend," said the king. "Is there anything I can do for you?"

Ivan bowed low and asked the king if he would be prepared to accept a humble gift from him. So the carved bird changed hands.

When the king returned to his palace he made sure the little carving stood in a prominent place where everybody could see it. One of those who did was the palace carpenter – and he was disgusted.

"What on earth does his majesty want a very poor little carving like that there for? Why, for Christmas I'll make him the best carving of a bird anybody has ever seen – then everybody will admire it too."

So the palace carpenter got to work. Using all the fine tools at his disposal he carved a huge, magnificent eagle. Then carrying this enormous piece of work he asked if he might see the king, and a few hours later he was standing in front of his ruler.

"Your majesty," the carpenter said "I couldn't help noticing that very poor carving of a bird you have in the palace. If you will forgive me saying so I think you could have something more impressive." At that he handed King Boris his superb carving.

"Thank you," said the king. "This really is an outstanding piece of work, would you please stand it under the carving of the small bird."

"But ... your majesty," spluttered the carpenter, "you mean you are still going to leave that poor little piece of work ... ?"

The king interrupted. "Your work deserves to be shown because it is a work of great skill, but it was given with pride. That small carving of a bird deserves an even higher place in my collection because it was given with love."

Notes

Follow up themes: giving and gifts; personal skills.

The theme of 'Gifts' is one which can be explored along a variety of lines in pre-Christmas work (time, skills, effort, music etc.) and there is even a carol of that title (*Gifts* – words and music by Olive Kershaw).

Two prayers which seem appropriate to this story are as follows:

1 When you help people, don't 'blow your own trumpet'. (*Matthew 6:2*)
2 *The second prayer is an adaptation of St. Ignatius' famous prayer:*
   Let us learn to:
   Give and not count the cost,
   Work and not look for rest
   Or always think about what is the reward.

82
Stockings and
Santa Claus

The idea of hanging up a stocking came from one of the many legends which portray Archbishop Nicholas of Myra (St Nicholas – Santa Claus) as a very generous man.

Everybody knows that if we hang stockings up on Christmas Eve we hope to get some presents in them. But how did this idea come about? Well, listen carefully …

"Oh dear, oh dear, oh dear, what shall I do?"

The man who said these words had lost all his money, and his three daughters were soon to be married. Now he had nothing at all to give them.

"Have you nothing left at all?" asked the man who was listening. This man's name was Nicholas and he was the Archbishop of a town called Myra, long ago.

"Nothing – nothing at all," wailed the distressed father.

Later that night when he went home Nicholas got to thinking. "Those poor girls," he thought. "Through no fault of their own they will have no money at all when they get married. If they had a little, how much easier it would be for them. Now, if I look at my money I'm sure I can spare enough to give them a little help."

So Nicholas went down to the cellar where he kept his gold. There he counted out three piles. Next he placed each pile in an identical purse and then tied the purses carefully.

By this time it was very late and the old town was dark and still. "It's just right for what I want to do," thought Nicholas. So closing his door quietly behind him he set off to walk through the silent streets.

"If I'm careful," he thought, "nobody will see me and those girls will have no idea where the money has come from – other than their father."

Eventually, the shadowy figure of the Archbishop reached the house where the three daughters lived. Looking up at it he saw the chimney standing out even in the darkness. Reaching into his pocket Nicholas took out the first purse and, taking careful aim, he threw it high in the air so that it fell down the chimney. Then he did the same with the second ... and the third.

Now what Nicholas didn't know was that inside the house, at the bottom of the chimney, a very big stocking had been left out to dry. As the purses bounced down the chimney they landed ... one ... two ... three ... in the stocking. Imagine the excitement next morning when each of the girls found a purse full of gold, with her name on it, tucked up in the stocking! Now they had enough money to pay for their weddings.

Notes

Follow up themes: generosity; gifts; traditions.

The original St Nicholas was Archbishop of Myra in Asia during the first part of the fourth century. He died on December 6th (a significant Christmas date in continental Europe) between 345 and 355. There are many legends about his friendly, unobtrusive generosity – one rather dramatic one when he plucked three small children from a tub in which they were being pickled to death.

A particularly appropriate Biblical reference to relate to the story here would be:
"When you do some act of charity, do not let your left hand know what your right hand is doing; your good deed must be secret." (*Matthew 6 : 3 – 4*)

Concluding prayer:
Let us think this morning of how the figure of St Nicholas – or Santa Claus – fills our minds with thoughts of joy, fun and excitement. Let us pray that children less fortunate that us may be given the gift of hope this Christmas. Amen.

83
An Austrian Christmas

Christmas in another country – seen through the eyes of a child – emphasises the joy of the occasion.

"I can hardly believe I'm here," thought Jessica to herself, as the car climbed up the road into the high, snow laden mountains.

"We'll soon be home now," said Inge, interrupting Jessica's thoughts. Inge was Jessica's cousin, and the two girls were spending Christmas at Inge's house in the mountains of Austria.

The days leading up to Christmas Eve slipped away quickly and the two girls spent a long time making the manger which they were going to take round other houses on this night. Finally it was ready.

"Now, as soon as all the other girls get here we'll go," said Inge.

"What happens exactly?" asked Jessica.

"You'll see," replied Inge. "Ah, here they are now."

So the group of girls set off round the village. They carried the manger with them and 'showed the Christ Child' to the people in each house they called at. In between houses they sang Christmas carols.

"What's this?" asked Jessica suddenly, as she saw another group of people coming down the mountainside and singing beautifully.

"Oh, that's another custom we have," explained Inge. "The family who live farthest away from the church start out for their nearest neighbour's house. They carry torches and sing carols as they do so. Then their neighbours join them, as do the families from every house they call at. They all then make for the church."

Jessica looked at the long line of people, warm in their heavy coats, each carrying a torch and each singing heartily. This Christmas in Austria was even better than she thought it would be and reminded her of how many people, all over the world, were celebrating the birth of Jesus.

Notes

Follow up themes: Christmas around the world.

A useful support for this assembly would be a recording of a brass band playing carols as background music. This could then be linked to further comment on another Austrian Christmas Eve tradition – 'Turmblasen'. This is the playing of choral music by brass instruments in the steeples of local churches.

Concluding prayer:
Let us give thanks for Christmas – a time when so many different people all over the world celebrate the birth of Jesus. Let us pray that the peace and goodwill of this time is carried on into the days, weeks and months which follow. Amen.

84
The horse

We can't expect to be seen in a good light at Christmas if we spend the rest of the year behaving badly.

Oscar had been a soldier. What's more, he had been a cavalry soldier and gone to war on a magnificent horse. Oscar's horse was called Captain, and in his soldiering days nothing had been too good for Captain. He was well fed, beautifully groomed and kept as warm and dry as possible.

"After all," said Oscar, "a soldier is only as good as his horse."

But Oscar's soldiering days had come to an end and, sad to say, he now treated Captain very differently. Any old scraps of food would do for him, day after day he was worked too hard, and often he was tethered in the wind and the rain. Captain grew thinner and weaker, his body was covered with sores and his coat was threadbare.

One year, as Christmas approached, Oscar heard that there was to be a grand Christmas parade through the village where he lived.

"Yes!" replied Oscar, when he was asked to take part. "I'll dress up as Father Christmas and Captain can pull me on a sleigh through the village. I'll like that."

When he got home that night Oscar brought Captain into the barn and started grooming him. Great tufts came out of the poor horse's already sparse coat. Instead of the scraps of chaff which was the usual fare, Captain was given the finest quality oats, but they were now too rich for him. Finally when Oscar put him between the shafts of the sleigh the poor old horse was too weak to pull it.

"So," thought Captain sadly, as he looked at his frustrated master. "By your neglect and bad treatment you've turned me from a magnificent horse into a tired ass and you can't turn me back to a horse again with just one day's good treatment.

(Based on an Aesop's fable)

Notes

Follow up themes: 'Not just at Christmas – but all the year.'

This story could promote plenty of discussion – with the RSPCA slogan: 'A dog is for life, not just for Christmas' – as a useful parallel to draw on.

Concluding prayer:

Let us remember this morning some words by a very famous writer called Charles Dickens. He said: "There seems a magic in the very name of Christmas. Petty jealousies and discords are forgotten – would that Christmas lasted the whole year through."

Let us try to behave all through the year with the kindness and friendliness we try to show, and hope to receive, at Christmas. Amen.

85
A fair exchange

What are the really important things in life? This story gives us a reminder.

Long ago a small girl called Elizabeth was making her way home from a Christmas party. She had been give a doll as a present at the party and she was delighted with it. As she walked through the thick wood which led to her home it began to snow heavily.

She found that she could only move very slowly and eventually she sat down, quite exhausted. Instantly, an old woman appeared before her.

"If you will give me that doll I will give you a magic bottle which you can never drink dry," said the old woman.

"No thank you, I would rather keep my present," replied the girl politely.

Then, clicking her fingers, the old woman made a beautiful party dress appear in front of Elizabeth. "Well, now you can have the bottle *and* this lovely party dress in exchange for that doll."

"Sorry," said Elizabeth. "I just want to keep my doll."

"How about this then?" Again the old woman snapped her fingers. This time two life sized dolls and a puppy appeared in the snow.

"It's no use," sighed Elizabeth. "Thank you for all your offers but I would rather keep my Christmas present than have anything else."

"Well," went on the old woman, "I'm afraid I have some bad news for you. Whilst you have been away from home your mother has become very ill. The only thing that can save her life is a handful of this special snow I am holding in my hand. Will you give me your doll for this handful of snow?"

"Yes, oh yes," cried Elizabeth. "If you will make my mother better please take the doll at once and help me to get home as quickly as possible!"

The old woman smiled. "Take the snow my child – and keep your present. Fortunate will be the people who know you in their lives."

Notes

Follow up themes: mothers; gifts.

This story might provide an opportunity to talk about Mary, mother of Jesus. Mary was a native of Nazareth whose parents were possibly Joachim and Anna. Both have been venerated as saints and it is particularly interesting to note that Anna is the patron saint of midwives. Various religious paintings show Mary weaving when receiving the visit of an angel who told her of the momentous events which were forthcoming.

Concluding prayer:

Let us give thanks this Christmas for all mothers, remembering the love and care which they unselfishly give us. Amen.

86
Carols

The stories behind the carols add further interest to them.

"They are *very* good."

So said Queen Victoria as she listened to the group of singers who had come all the way from America to give some concerts in England. One particularly interesting thing about the 'Jubilee Singers', as they were called, was that they were first formed by freed slaves. Then the children of the freed slaves joined and so the tradition continued.

Although they were now free, and although they were wonderful singers, the group still had many hard times, when they weren't allowed to stay in certain hotels because they were black. Some years after the Jubilee Singers were formed they started to sing a carol which has become a favourite of many children in British primary schools. It is : 'Go tell it on the mountain'.

Another carol which we sing at Christmas is 'While shepherds watched their flocks by night'. This was written by an Irishman called Nahum Tate who was born in 1652 and became a very famous poet in England. Although this carol must have been sung millions of times all over the world since then, Nahum Tate died in London in desperate poverty in 1715.

The lady who wrote 'In the bleak mid-winter' was also a poet. Her name was Christina Rossetti, and she was so beautiful that many artists wanted to use her as a model when they painted. Two of the most famous artists of the time did this. Their names were Millais and Holman Hunt.

Then there is a popular carol, 'Mary had a baby'. Nobody knows who wrote this but we do know that it comes from a tiny island called St Helena. This island is covered in mountains, is between Africa and South America – a very long way from Bethlehem!

A less well known carol is the one called 'Hark the glad sound' but an interesting thing about it is that is was written by a man called Philip Doddridge who was born in 1702 and was the youngest of twenty children!

These facts show us that the carols we sing at Christmas come from far and wide and have been written by many different kinds of people. This reminds us of Christmas itself, a festival enjoyed and celebrated all over the world by people of many races and languages.

Notes

Follow up themes: carols; Christmas in other countries; music.

For those teachers who want to pursue this theme in more depth then a very useful book is *Christmas carols and their stories* by Christopher Idle (Lion).

The following prayer could be used to end the service:

Let us give thanks this morning for those clever people who compose songs which we enjoy listening to and singing. Let us give particular thanks for the talents of the writers of Christmas carols, which give so much pleasure to so many people at this time of year. Amen.

87
The last tree

Christmas is a time which should be enjoyed by people of all ages.

"Christmas is for young people – at least it doesn't seem to be for me." Old Joe Garland said the words to himself for about the hundredth time. Pushed and jostled by the people in the Christmas Eve crowd doing their last minute shopping, he put his case down on the pavement and flexed his tired hand.

Of course he was grateful to Doris for insisting that he come and spend Christmas with them. And she and Martin were always very kind. And his grandchildren seemed pleased to see him – but somehow he still felt an outsider, a sort of relic from a time past. Oh yes, they thanked him for their presents, and always gave him theirs, but nothing he did seemed important anymore.

As he stood there, like an island with the tide of people surging round him, he noticed that he was beside a stall selling Christmas trees. Fine trees – at a fine price of course – were being sold and bundled away. Then he noticed a rather sad specimen. Lying half on its side, smaller than the others, it was reached over by anxious hands grasping for bigger, taller, better trees.

"Bit like me that one," thought Joe, and picked up his case.

When he got to Doris' house there was the usual Christmas Eve excitement. The children had waited up to give him a goodnight kiss before they went to bed. Martin arrived just as they had gone.

"Hello Dad," he said. "Nice to see you ... y'know, Doris, we're not going to get one. The shops are closing and ..."

"But Martin, we can't ..."

"Anything I can do to help?" asked Joe.

"No Dad," replied Doris. "The man who was going to deliver our Christmas tree has let us down, and Martin can't find one left anywhere."

"Have you tried the lane by the station?" asked Joe.

"No," muttered Martin absently. "It'll be no good anyway. I've tried everywhere else and there's just nothing left."

"Right, well let me have a go," said Joe.

"But Dad ..." Doris began to protest, but Joe was already shrugging back into his coat.

Forgetting about how tired he felt, he stepped out over the crisp, flattened snow back in the direction he had come from just a few minutes earlier. The crowds were much thinner now and Joe felt a pang of uncertainty as he turned the corner where the stall had been.

The stall holder was just packing up. A Ford van had been backed up the street and two men were dismantling the stall and putting the pieces into the back of the van. The tree lay flat on the ground, surviving trampling feet only by good luck.

Joe hurried towards the scene. "I say – that one tree you've got left there. How much do you want for it?"

One of the men stopped and looked round in surprise. "This one?" He picked up the tree as if he couldn't believe anybody would be interested in such a sorry specimen.

"Yes," replied Joe.

"It's yours, Grandad – take it free – and Merry Christmas."

When Joe got back to Doris and Martin's he left the tree outside in the back garden. They were busy wrapping presents when he went in.

"I got one," he said breathlessly.

"Oh Dad you've saved the day," gasped Doris.

Martin clapped him on the back.

"Can I ask you a favour?" queried Joe.

"Fire away," Martin replied.

"Well," said Joe, "when you've wrapped the presents and put the tree decorations out ... will you leave me to put the tree up and ... well ... arrange everything?"

Doris looked at her father strangely. Then Martin squeezed her arm. "Of course we will Dad. We're finished anyway. You know where the box of sand is to wedge it in and ..."

"Yes, yes," answered Joe, anxious for them to go.

Soon he was by himself in the flickering light of the fire. The pile of presents stood in readiness by the settee and the box of decorations stood unopened on top of the television set. After getting the box of sand from the kitchen and arranging the gaily coloured wrapping paper round it, Joe went out for the tree.

As he picked it up he felt a strange sense of excitement. Somehow the tree didn't seem so bedraggled now. It even seemed to have grown in the short time it had been propped up beside the back wall of the house.

Pushing the base into the sand and wedging it with the bricks Joe began easing the branches up all round the tree. To his surprise, none of them was broken and, as he pushed and shaped, they straightened firmly into place, their greenness spreading out into the room and seeming to invite the adornments which waited in the box.

It was two hours before Joe was finished. The light from the fire died to a warm glow but it was enough to show the tree in all its glory. Glistening with baubles and tinsel, a fairy on top and with presents piled round its base, it seemed to be poised in readiness for Joe to test the colourful lights which were interspersed amongst its branches. Joe reached towards the electric point in the wall and pushed in the plug.

As the light sparked through the greenery, throwing shadows on the wall and bathing the room in a warm and magic light, a distant clock began to chime midnight. Joe sat on the floor of the quiet room. It was Christmas. He thought of the words that had been going through his head when he had first seen the tree.

"No," he said aloud. "Christmas is for the young – and the old as well; Christmas is for everybody."

Notes

Follow up themes: families; old people; needs at Christmas.

Useful address: Age Concern, 54 Knatchbull Road, London SE5 9QU.

Useful Bible reference: 'Pass no judgement and you will not be judged; do not condemn and you will not be condemned; ... give and gifts will be given to you ...' (*Luke 6, 37-38*)

Christmas at its best is a time of beauty as well as love. For a thought provoking prayer which could engender lots of follow up discussion there is an old Chinese proverb which could be used here. It is simple but its point is far reaching.

'If you have two loaves sell one and buy a lily.'

VI

Stories for other festive occasions

(*Note* With regard to festivals of other cultures which change from year to year it is necessary to consult a document such as the *Calendar of Religious Festivals* which is produced annually by the SHAP Working Party, The National Society's RE Centre, 23 Kensington Square, London, W8 5HN.)

88
The time the harvest failed

There are many points which can be followed up in this story but, most of all, it emphasises the real kindness of people who give when they have very little to give.

Walter looked the small loaf of bread on the shelf.

"That's to feed five of us," he thought, "and now that the harvest has failed where on earth are we going to get the next one from?"

Jane, Walter's wife, saw her husband looking at the last of the bread she had baked. She too knew what a disaster the failure of the harvest had been.

"Come on, come on," she said, "something will turn up. Let's share this out with the children now."

A few minutes later the desperately poor family were sitting round the table. Walter and Jane had two small pieces of bread in front of them, and their three children each had a slightly bigger piece. Before anyone had taken a bite there was a knock on the door.

"Sir, I've been travelling for days and I'm desperately hungry," mumbled the thin, tired looking man who stood in the doorway when Walter answered the knock.

"Come in my friend," replied Walter immediately. "We've precious little but you're welcome to share what we have."

"Thank you," replied the stranger, putting the bundle he carried over his shoulder down on the floor.

"Thank you," he said again as he hungrily ate the piece of bread Walter offered him.

"You must be really starving," said Jane, as she watched Walter's bread disappear. "Take my piece too."

Once again the stranger ate hungrily and, so sorry were Walter and Jane for him, they offered him the children's bread too.

"I'm sorry," said Walter after this, "but I'm afraid that's every bit of food we have in the house."

"You have nothing else?" queried the stranger. Once again Walter shook his head.

"Well now," went on the stranger, suddenly seeming to be less frail and tired, "you gave me everything you possessed because you thought I was in need. Now let's share what I've got."

So saying the mysterious visitor bent down, lifted up and opened his bundle. The eyes of his hosts widened in amazement as he brought out bread and fruit of every kind. Piling his delicious fare onto the table he invited everyone to eat.

Walter, Jane and their children ate as never before and the food tasted every bit as delicious as it looked. What's more, no matter how much they ate the pile of food never seemed to get any less.

(*This is a very free adaptation of a story from the Hindu epic, the Mahabharata.*)

Notes

Follow up themes: harvest; gifts; appearances.

A possible quotation for expanding thought on this theme is:

If you shut your ears when people cry for help, when you cry for help no-one will hear you. (*Proverbs 21:13*)

Concluding prayer:

Let us pray this morning for the strength to be generous when we don't feel like being so. Let us remember that there are many things we can give – time, effort, a kind word. Let us pray that we can always act in the way we would like other people to act towards us. Amen.

89
Will you marry me?
(Harvest)

Apples play a very important part in this story so it is a useful one to relate to harvest time. The main theme of this Greek myth, however, shows how very different people can live happily together.

King Schoenus wanted his daughter Atalanta to get married and have a son. Now Atalanta had had a very strange life. When she was a child she had been abandoned in the mountains and brought up by bears. As a result she was immensely strong as well as very beautiful.

"I will only get married on one condition," said Atalanta.

"Oh – and what's that?" queried her father.

"I will only marry a man who can beat me in a running race."

Now there was no shortage of men who wanted to marry the beautiful princess, but she was the most fantastic runner and she beat one after another. One day yet another young man arrived and asked to marry Atalanta.

"You know what you have to do?" asked King Schoenus.

"Yes your majesty."

"Well you don't look much like a runner to me."

"Oh I'm not, I'm not very good at all really."

"Well then – you'll be wasting all our time," said the king impatiently.

"I don't think so," replied Hipponemes (that was the young man's name). "I've prepared very carefully."

So the king granted his bad tempered approval and yet another cross country race was organised … and began.

Naturally Atalanta raced away into an early lead but, approaching a tree, she saw a magnificent ripe red apple fall from it.

"Hmm, shame to waste such a beauty," thought Atalanta, "and it looks as if I can win this without much effort at all."

So Atalanta paused to eat the splendid apple. A little further on the same thing happened. Every time she built up a lead in the race another tempting and lovely apple would fall in her path. As a result Atalanta didn't run anything like as well as she usually did – and Hipponemes won the race.

After it was all over Atalanta realised something ...

"Those apples didn't just fall where they did by accident," she thought. "The whole thing was arranged by Hipponemes ... well, if he was prepared to go to all that much trouble it just shows how much he wants to marry me, and how clever he is to work out a way to win the race."

So the beautiful athlete Atalanta, and the quiet, shrewd Hipponemes were married – and made each other, and King Schoenus, very happy!

Notes

Follow up themes: determination; planning ahead; caring.

Apples are a dominant feature of harvest time and particularly relevant to this story is the old custom that when a son was born an apple tree was planted by the family.

Harvest Festivals in schools seem mainly to be in late September now ('September blow soft, Till the fruit's in the loft' – Thomas Constable) and this theme could be the starting point for a suitable prayer.

Dear God, Thank you for the harvest and we pray that it may be gathered safely in. Let us think too about all those people in the world for whom there is not a harvest and not enough to eat.

We pray that they can be helped as much as possible by as many people as possible in every way possible. Amen.

(Photographs readily supplied by such as Christian Aid/Oxfam etc. could be on display to supplement this prayer.)

90
Catherine
(Guy Fawkes' night)

Bonfire night gives us the opportunity to remember one of the bravest of Christian saints – and the woman whose name is used in the firework – 'Catherine wheel'.

"No, no matter how many times he asks me to marry him, I won't."

"But Catherine, this is no ordinary man we are talking about, this is an Emperor!"

"I don't care about that, the answer is still no."

So saying, Catherine turned away from her friend. She was a young and very beautiful princess who lived in Alexandria, a great port in Egypt. The person who wanted to marry her was Maxentius the Roman Emperor, who ruled over the province where she lived. Again he came to see the beautiful princess.

"But why won't you marry me?" he asked.

"Well, for a start ," replied Catherine, "you are having Christians put to death – and I am a Christian."

"Ah," said the pagan Emperor, "but don't you see, the Christians are trouble makers. They're dangerous and I want this to be a peaceful state so, they are best out of the way. But ... I wouldn't dream of having you killed. I want you to be my wife and to be rich and powerful and have everything you want."

"I'm sorry, your majesty," said Catherine, with bowed head. "But I'd rather die than be your wife. You see, I know what it means to be a Christian."

So, once more frustrated, the Emperor went back to his palace. After some hours of thought he sent for his three wisest men. They listened carefully to the instructions he gave them.

"You are to go and see Catherine," ordered Maxentius. "You are to use all your wit and smooth words to persuade her to give up this Christian nonsense and become my wife. Think of the life she'll have if she does this! Now go – and arrange it."

The three wise men didn't think this would be a difficult task. After all it was no fun being a Christian now Maxentius had decided to get rid of them. They were bullied and tracked down and hunted wherever they were. Sooner or later this would happen to Catherine, but all she had to do to stop this was to become the Emperor's wife. That should be a simple enough choice!

Eventually the three men met with the princess. "Can we have a talk to you?" they said.

"Of course," replied Catherine, and listened carefully to all they had to say. When they had finished she spoke.

"Now," she said quietly, "will you listen to what I have to say."

Catherine then went on to tell the three men what it meant to be a Christian, how her belief gave her such strength and how she must help others all she could. As she talked the three wise men listened with increasing interest. Finally she finished and the first man nodded his head slowly.

"You're right," he said very slowly and carefully.

"Absolutely right," agreed the second … and the third.

"We must go back and tell Maxentius he's making a great mistake," went on the first man, "at once."

So the three men returned to the Emperor's palace and sought an audience with Maxentius. He was naturally anxious to see them and hear what they had to say. When the leader of the group began to speak Maxentius could hardly believe his ears. The men he had sent to persuade Catherine to change her mind were now back trying to persuade him to change his. He was absolutely furious and roared to the man to stop. It didn't end there of course. Guards were summoned and the three men were sent to prison and killed. Now Maxentius sent for Catherine again.

"This time," he said to her, "I want you to realise that you are under arrest. Unless you agree to marry me now you will be put to death like other Christians. And – I'll make an example of you by making you die on those wheels."

As he said this he pointed to four spiked wheels between which Catherine was to be bound. When they turned their various ways she would die a terrible death.

Now of course Maxentius didn't really want to kill Catherine. He just wanted her to do what he said and he thought that this might frighten her into doing just that. However, to his astonishment, she again firmly refused to give up her Christianity. So the furious Emperor ordered her to be put on the wheels, and the turning to begin.

Then a fantastic thing happened. Just as the terrible wheels were about to turn and do their dreadful work a mysterious burst of flame destroyed them totally – and freed Catherine.

Sadly, this part of the story did not end happily there. Astonished though he was, the cruel and unforgiving Emperor had Catherine immediately killed with a sword.

However, that was not really the end of the story. Thousands and thousands of people had heard about Catherine's bravery and this gave them the strength and determination to go on being Christian themselves no matter what the difficulties. And so on Bonfire Night when we light the fireworks called Catherine wheels, we are remembering the courage of a young princess who died one thousand six hundred years ago.

Notes

Follow up themes: what people believe; courage; selfishness; determination.

The spiked wheel is the symbol of St Catherine, along with a book to show her learning, a crown to show her royal descent and a palm branch to show her martyrdom.

A useful Bible quotation here is: There is no greater love than this, that man should lay down his life for his friends. *John 15:13*

Concluding prayer:

Let us think this morning about what people believe. Let us learn to be tolerant and understanding of others, and to be able to listen to all points of view. Amen.

91
Found out!

(New Year)

This old African folk tale is a useful one with which to start the Spring Term when New Year resolutions are still in the air!

All the animals in the jungle were going to a funeral. There they all were in a long line, the rat, the deer, the elephant, the monkey, the leopard.

Now at this time the leopard was much the same as he is today – except for the fact that he had no spots. As he walked along with all the other animals he suddenly spotted a farm near to the track they were on.

"I'm starving," the leopard thought to himself. "I think I'll just slip into this farm and see what there is to eat – and then catch the others up."

So the leopard crept stealthily into the farm, and ate his fill of everything in sight. Having done so he bounded off to catch the others. No sooner had he left the farm than the farmer arrived back and saw that somebody had stolen nearly all his food.

"It must be one of that long line of animals I've just passed," he thought. "Well, I'm not standing for this."

So saying the farmer chased after the animals and brought them all to a stop.

"One of you is a thief," he cried. "A thief who has just raided my farm for food."

"No – not us," said the animals one after the other, because of course no-one had actually seen the leopard slink away to do his thieving.

"Well in that case, if you're all innocent, you won't mind me giving you a test to prove it," went on the farmer. The animals agreed, and the farmer lit a fire in a hole in the ground.

"Now," he said. "I want you all to jump over that. If you're innocent it will be easy – but the guilty one will fall in."

Some of the smaller animals were rather frightened, but their innocence gave them extra strength and they jumped the fire easily. Finally, only the leopard was left.

"It's a simple jump for him," mumbled a small rat.

"It certainly is," agreed the deer, "and then we'll all be proved innocent."

The leopard prepared to jump. To the animals' surprise he appeared nervous. Now we will never know whether it was a guilty conscience or a too full stomach, but he made an absolute mess of the jump – and landed plumb in the fire.

With a howl of pain he scrambled out and rolled in the grass to put the flames out. As he did so big brown and black spots appeared on his body where he had been burnt – and from that day on the leopard carried these spots.

(Adapted from an African folk tale)

Notes

Follow up themes: honesty; temptation; being found out.

An obvious talking point from this story is that even if nobody else knows we have done something wrong – we do ourselves. To support this one of the sayings of Philo Judaeus, a Jew famous for his theological writing, could be used here: 'You should want to be good just for the sake of being good.'

Concluding prayer:

As we start a new term and a new year let us think about the many mistakes we made last year. We pray that we have learned from these, and be given the strength to make fewer this year. Amen.

92
The Musicians of Bremen
(April 1st)

On the one hand this old story can claim to be suitable tale for April 1st because of its fun and trickery. At another level however it is a story of 'never giving up'.

The four of them were on the way to Bremen – and what a group they made. There was the donkey, worn out by long years of carrying, and the dog who was now too old and slow to hunt. They were joined by the cat whose teeth had gone so blunt he could no longer catch mice, and the cock who had just escaped being included in a recipe for soup.

"But," said the donkey, speaking for all of them, "we may be old, but we'll be musicians when we get to Bremen!"

Full of enthusiasm the four friends started on their long journey. They travelled slowly but determinedly for one long day – and then saw a cottage ahead of them.

"It would be nice if we could rest there for the night," said the cat. "Go and have a look through the window, donkey, and tell us what you see."

A few minutes later the donkey hobbled back and spoke excitedly. "Fantastic!" he said. "You should just see the food on the table in there! But the bad news is the room is full of robbers."

"If we could get them out ..." began the dog.

"... we could enjoy a feast," continued the cat.

The friends worked out a plan.

Minutes later they were ready. The donkey stood outside the window, the dog was on his back, and the cat was on top of the dog. Perched on top of the cat was the cock.

"Right," called out the cock, "let's make music!"

At once a terrible cacophony of braying, barking, meowing and crowing broke out – and the friends jumped through the window into the cottage.

The robbers got such a terrific fright that they bolted through the door and ran off into the woods as fast as they could. At once the four friends set about the feast and ate their fill. Then, as each one was satisfied, the donkey went out to sleep in the yard, the dog settled down by the door, the cat on the hearth and the cock on a rafter. Darkness fell and all was peace in the cottage.

Meanwhile …

"It's dark in there now," said the chief of the robbers, who had crept back to the edge of the woods to look at the cottage.

"I reckon we've been scared by nothing much, and I'm going back to have a look."

So saying the chief of the robbers went back to the cottage and crept inside. Tip-toeing through the room he stepped on the cat who at once leapt at him. Terrified again the robber dashed for the door – only to be bitten by the dog as he did so. Staggering outside he was just in time to be kicked by the donkey, whilst the cock screeched louder than ever.

The robber ran for his life – and when he reached the woods his men dashed after him. When they were a mile away they stopped and the chief gasped out his story.

"Terrible, terrible it was," he spluttered, "a witch scratched my face, a man stuck a knife in my leg as I ran by the door and a monster in the yard hit me with a club. Whilst all this was going on a judge on the roof screeched – 'Bring him to me!' We're never going back there."

So the robbers fled and the friends enjoyed their new house so much that they stayed there for ever.

(Adapted from the Brothers Grimm)

Notes

Follow up themes: old people; never give up; fun.

A most appropriate Biblical reference for this story – and indeed for this occasion is as follows:

'I know that there is nothing good for man except to be happy and live the best life he can while he is alive. However, that a man should eat and drink and enjoy himself, in return for all his labours, is a gift of God. A merry heart keeps a man alive, and joy lengthens the span of his days.' *Ecclesiastes 3: 12-14; 30:22*

Concluding prayer:

Let us give thanks this morning for people everywhere who are fun to be with and make us laugh. Amen.

93
Giving
(Easter)

There is an old saying: 'To give is better than to receive'. Apart from Christmas probably the most famous day of the year for giving is Maundy Thursday.

"Isn't it marvellous to be here?" whispered the man.

"Yes, to be invited to Westminster Abbey is wonderful," replied the lady next to him.

"Sshh you two, here's the queen."

The long line of men and women waited with growing excitement as the queen came towards them. It was Maundy Thursday, the Thursday before Easter Day, and they had been invited to Westminster Abbey to receive a present from the queen.

Soon she was moving along the line giving three purses to each person. The men got a red purse and two white ones, and the ladies got a green one, a red one and a white one. Each purse contained specially minted Maundy Money.

After the service the man and woman who had been talking together before the queen arrived caught a bus home together.

"You know," said the man, "that service has been going on since the year 600 AD and ever since then the king or queen has given Maundy Money, or in earlier times, gifts to the poor people."

"When you say gifts, what do you mean?" asked the woman.

"Well, in Queen Elizabeth's I's time, for instance, she gave the poor people a hamper each. This hamper was a sort of wicker basket called a 'Maund'."

"That's interesting, but what was in the 'Maund'?"

"Well, in Queen Elizabeth's time there was some money, some fish, cloth to make some clothes, something to drink, an apron and a towel."

"A towel?"

"Yes, because you see earlier kings and queens not only gave the poor presents but they washed their feet too."

"Goodness me," said the woman. "Here's my stop coming up, but quickly, tell me one more thing, how many people does the queen choose each year?"

"Ah, that's easy," said the man with a smile. "The number of men and women to receive Maundy presents is always the same as the number in the queen's age."

"Well, I'll never forget this Maundy Thursday," sighed the woman as she got up to leave. "Goodbye."

Notes

Follow up themes: giving; rich and poor; customs.

Easter is of course the time of a great gift when life is revived and renewed – symbolised by the lighting of the Easter Candle.

The following prayer could be used to end the service:
Let us think this morning about the great gift we have been given in our lives. Let us give thanks for our senses which enable us to appreciate so much that is beautiful in the world. Let us give thanks for the love, companionship and friendship of our family and friends. Amen.

94
The homecoming
(Easter)

Hot cross buns are one of the great traditions of Easter. The story which follows reminds us of how much our mothers love us.

It was Good Friday and Jane looked out of the windows of her house towards the River Thames. She was a widow who had only one son, and he was a sailor.

"He's coming home today!"

She was so happy that she sang the words aloud even though she was alone. "He's coming home today!"

She then made her way to the oven and looked inside. There, rising nicely, was a special hot cross bun which she was baking for this day which was so special for her.

Jane sang to herself as the morning sped away. She knew her son's ship was due to dock at midday and he would soon be here at their home near London's dockland. It was shortly after 1 o'clock when there was a knock at the door.

Rushing to open it, she suddenly paused. A knock ... John wouldn't knock on his own door would he? With a sense of rising panic she opened the door.

A stranger stood there, twisting his hat nervously in his hand. "Mrs Wilkins?"

"Yes."

"Er ... I've got some bad news I'm afraid."

"John!"

"Well, we've heard his ship went down off the coast during the night."

"But ... were there any survivors? Wasn't anybody saved? What about John?"

"Well ... nobody really knows you see. Nobody saw her sink, but there's no news of anybody being saved. I'm terribly sorry but ..." The poor seaman stood there, miserable at having to deliver such a sad message.

Jane reached out and squeezed his shoulder. Then she went inside and sat down. "He might have got ashore somewhere," she thought to herself, "and if he did, when he gets home he'll be hungry."

So saying she got out the hot cross bun and put it on a large plate in the middle of the table.

Sadly John did not come that day, or the next or the next, or ...

But Jane never gave up hope and, every year, she baked a special hot cross bun just in case her son would turn up.

Now this story took place a long time ago, but it has a strange ending. When the widow died, her house was knocked down and a pub was built in its place. Obviously the pub is near the river and many sailors use it. Every Easter, on Good Friday, the landlord asks a sailor to put a newly baked hot cross bun in a hanging basket ... just in case ...

Notes

Follow up themes: hope; mothers; traditions; families.

The cross on hot cross buns is now associated with the Christian Easter, but it almost certainly originates from pre-Christian times. Women baked 'magic' wheat cakes for the pagan spring festival and two of these (complete with crosses on them) were found in the ruins of Herculaneum after the eruption of Vesuvius in 79AD.

Two prayers which might be used to end this assembly are:

Easter is a time to pause ... then to stop and think ... beyond. (G. Simpson)

Let us think again about this story, and how it reminds us of the love mothers have for their children. Let us give thanks for our mothers, and try to be all that they hope we might be. Amen.

95
St Peter's Day
(June 29th)

The story of Peter's final stand for his Christian beliefs inspired thousands of his fellow believers.

"It's burning, I tell you – look it's burning!"

"You're right, look at those flames! Quick, run or we'll be burnt alive!"

All over the great city of Rome men and women were calling out in panic and terror. A huge fire had broken out and was sweeping through the streets, burning all before it. For six days the fire raged and then, when it finally died down and people drifted back into the city, they were met with depressing sights. Spirals of smoke hailed up into the sky above the wreckage of more than three quarters of the city's houses. Thousands and thousands of people no longer had homes. They were angry.

"Somebody should be made to pay for this!"

"The Emperor – he's supposed to be in charge!"

"Yes – and what was he doing while the place burned?"

Nero, the Roman Emperor, had all this unrest reported to him and he was worried. "What we need," he said to his minister, "is someone to blame the disaster on. That will make life easier for us and ... wait, just a minute, I've got it! We'll blame the Christians, then we can kill two birds with one stone."

Nero, like many Romans, hated the Christians. This seemed like a marvellous opportunity to get rid of them. Scores of arrests were made and Christians began to be tortured and killed.

At this time Peter, Jesus' great friend and disciple, was living in Rome. Two women, who were the wives of important Roman officials but were also Christians, came to see him.

"Peter, you are the most important Christian," said Albinus, "you must get away or you will be killed."

"But ..." began Peter.

"No but," interrupted Agrippa, the other woman. "Who can carry on spreading the great message better than you? You must escape."

So, secretly and at night, Peter slipped through the gates of the city. He avoided the soldiers easily and had made a good distance away when he stopped for a rest. As he dozed he imagined that he was talking to Jesus again!

"Hello Peter."

"Lord!"

"I'm sorry I can't stay. I'm going to Rome. I'm going to be crucified again."

Peter woke up with a start. He knew instantly what his dream meant. How could he have allowed himself to be persuaded to leave when other Christians there were suffering so badly?

Getting briskly to his feet he set off back to the city. As Albinus and Agrippa had feared, he was immediately arrested, and put to death. But when Christians heard what he had done, the story of his faith and courage spread far and wide. More and more people began to believe that being a Christian was the way that they wanted to live their lives.

Notes

Follow up themes: faith; courage; doing what we know is right.

This legend of Peter's death ends with his crucifixion (upside down at his request because he considered himself unworthy to be killed the same way as Jesus) and subsequent burial in Rome. The Emperor Constantine was supposed to have built a cathedral over the grave many years later – St Peter's Cathedral.

A relevant quotation from St Luke could be linked with this story:

"When a man has been given much, much will be expected of him; and the more a man has entrusted to him the more he will be required to pay." *Luke 12: 48*

Concluding prayer:

Let us think about St Peter in our prayers this morning. His nickname was 'the Rock'. Let us pray that as people we can be rock like and reliable in all our dealings with others. Amen.

96
The Queen's necklace
(Divali)

This is the story of a young woman who used her brains to make her family successful.

It all started with the queen's necklace.

"Where can it be? I've looked everywhere." The queen sighed with exasperation.

"The last time I saw it was on your window sill, your majesty," said one of her servants respectfully.

"Well it's not there now!" snapped the queen.

Meanwhile, a few miles from the palace a young woman was cleaning outside the door of her house when she saw a dead snake lying on the ground. She was just about to bury it when she saw a hawk flying overhead. Something was dangling from its beak. "I wonder what that is?" she thought. "Well, I know how I can find out."

Bending down she picked up the dead snake and threw it onto the roof of the cottage where she and her family lived. The hawk saw this and circled round.

Dakshina (that was the young woman's name) could almost see the hawk's mind working. That was a lovely juicy meal lying on the roof ... but he already had something in his mouth ... so ... The hawk made a sudden decision. Swooping down he dropped what was in his mouth, snatched up the dead snake and flew away to have a feast.

"Ah," gasped Dakshina as she saw what the hawk had dropped. It was a fabulous gold necklace.

Just at that moment her husband Ashrin and her father-in-law Kanwal Singh arrived home from work.

"Terrible fuss at the palace today I heard," said Ashrin.

"Yes," continued Kanwal Singh. "Queen's been in a dreadful mood – lost her favourite and most precious necklace I believe."

"Really," muttered Dakshina, not saying anything about her find.

That night Dakshina thought long and hard. She and Ashrin and Kanwal Singh were desperately poor – but they hadn't always been. In fact Kanwal Singh had been a king not very far away. Then he had offended Lakshmi, the goddess of wealth, and she had caused him to lose his kingdom.

"I wonder ... ," thought Dakshina, "I wonder."

The next day she went to see the queen.

"It's mine! It's mine! It's my beautiful necklace," gasped the queen excitedly, when Dakshina showed what she had brought.

"Oh thank you," went on the queen. "Now – a reward. You must have a reward. What would you like?"

"Well your majesty," said Dakshina slowly, it's nearly time for the great festival of Divali. I would like the yard of my house to be the only place where people can light lamps when the festival arrives. Everywhere else must stay dark."

The queen was shocked. She knew how everybody liked to light lamps to attract Lakshmi, goddess of wealth, to their homes when it was Divali. Still, she had made a promise, ... so ...

"Very well."

Shortly afterwards the great festival arrived and, as night fell, Lakshmi entered the kingdom. She was aghast – where were all the lights inviting her generosity? She was just beginning to get angry when she saw one house which was absolutely ablaze with lights, in the yard, shining through the windows, just everywhere. Lakshmi hurried towards this and knocked on the door.

Another surprise awaited her when the door opened and Dakshina stood there, but did not invite her in.

"Don't you know who I am?" asked the irritated Lakshmi. Usually, because they thought they were going to get money and luck from her people couldn't wait to invite her into their homes.

"I do," replied Dakshina, "but you took all out wealth away from us, why should I let you in?"

Now Lakshmi paused for thought. This was the only house around with lights welcoming her. If the other gods found out that she wasn't welcome here, well …

"Well, you'd better let me in and we'll see what we can do about all this," she said.

So Dakshina stood aside and the goddess came in, and was given a warm welcome. Later, when she departed, she left behind precious jewels of enormous value. With these Kanwal Singh got his kingdom back and he, Ashrin and Dakshina returned to where they belonged.

Whenever Dakshina saw a necklace after this she smiled a secret smile to herself.

(Adapted from an old Hindu story)

Notes

Follow up themes: quick thinking; money; lost and found.

Divali is the great Hindu festival of lights. (It takes place in October/November in the Western calendar.) This celebrates the triumph of Good over Evil, and is linked to the Rama and Sita story.

It is the time however when Lakshmi travels the Earth deciding upon where to stay a night and leave her gifts. Lakshmi is probably the most popular Hindu goddess because she also presides over love and luck. While she may leave great gifts however she is also fickle and can take as well as give.

Concluding prayer:
Let us think this morning about celebrations, when we can share with each other joy and laughter. Let us pause to think also of those whose lives are difficult and have little to celebrate. May they be given hope. Amen.

97
To help or not to help?
(Pentecost)

This story shows forcibly what might happen when we can offer help – but choose not to.

Isaac had a long journey to make to get his goods to market. The path was over long narrow mountain trails, and he divided his goods into two loads and put each of these on a donkey. The trio then set off.

Now, although Isaac wasn't sure of it, one donkey was stronger than the other and both donkeys knew this. The reason Isaac wasn't sure was because the weaker donkey always gave of his best and would never give up.

The two animals followed the man up ever steeper mountain paths. Sometimes they were so narrow that they were dangerous, at other times the donkeys could come alongside each other. After hours of travelling, when they were on a wide path, the weaker donkey spoke to his companion.

"Friend, I don't think I'm going to be able to make this climb without a bit of help. Could you take some of my burden until we get to the top? Then I'll take it back, and some of yours, when we're going downhill."

The stronger donkey looked across contemptuously. "We've got equal loads haven't we? Anyway, it's easier to carry stuff going down. Just get on with it and stop moaning. You'll get no help from me."

The weaker donkey carried on without a word. Higher and higher the group climbed, until eventually they were toiling up the narrowest path yet. Suddenly, the weaker donkey, exhausted to the point of collapse, missed his footing and fell from the path onto some boulders below. Anxiously Isaac scrambled down after him. But it was no good. The poor beast was dead.

"Ah, to lose one of my friends in such a way," groaned the merchant. "But still, life must go on."

So saying he dragged the complete load from the dead donkey's back and piled it onto the strong donkey. Such was the extra weight that the strong donkey's legs almost buckled and his back felt as if it would break.

"Oh – oh," he moaned to himself, worried and frightened. "If only I'd given him some help when he asked this would never have happened!" And he had to stagger down the long, long path carrying the whole load himself.

Notes

Follow up themes: help; sharing; strong and weak.

This story could be used in connection with the Jewish celebration of The Feast of Weeks (Pentecost) which commemorates the giving of the Ten Commandments on Mount Sinai. This feast is seven weeks after Passover and is also one of harvest.

In conjunction with the Torah's rules by which people should live, Leviticus 19 ('Love your neighbour as yourself') is particularly appropriate to this story.

Concluding prayer:

Let us think very carefully about this morning's story and hope that we can learn from it. We pray that we will help others wherever and whenever we can. Amen.

98
"I did it"
(Yom Kippur)

It is not always easy to tell the truth. Sometimes however telling the truth when it is difficult has surprising results.

"How many prisoners have you got here?" asked the general.

"About a hundred," replied the prison governor.

"I want to speak to them all – one at a time," went on the general.

"Of course sir," answered the governor.

He had heard of this new general who was ruling the country. Rumours said that he was one of the wisest men who ever lived.

"Hmm, I wonder about that," thought the governor to himself. "Why on earth does he want to talk to all of these prisoners, and by themselves at that?"

Aloud of course he said very different words. "I will make arrangements for you to talk to the prisoners immediately sir," he said.

For the rest of that day, and the next two days, the general spoke to the prisoners, and there were two more than a hundred to be exact!

"What is your name?" was the first question the general asked, and the second was, "Why are you here?"

Obviously the names were all different, but the answers to the second question had a certain sameness to them.

"What is your name?" "Isaac Rosen." "Why are you here?" "Well, they said I broke into a rich man's house and stole some jewellery – but it was all a mistake. I just called on him and when he was out I borrowed …"

"What is your name?" "Samuel Levine." "Why are you here?" "They say I nearly killed a man but it wasn't like that at all. I was just defending myself and I hardly …"

"What is your name?" "Joseph Strauss." "Why are you here?" "They said I burnt down my neighbour's house because he was much richer than me – but it was an accident – I swear it …"

So, hour after hour, the general heard the same thing. Every prisoner claimed that he was there by mistake. Whatever he had done was an accident, or he'd been forced to do it, or it was someone else who'd done it and he'd been blamed unjustly ... or ... or ... on and on went the excuses and claims of injustice.

Finally the general reached prisoner number 102.

"What is your name?"

"Jacob Fischer."

"Why are you here?"

"I stole three horses."

"Why?"

"Does it matter? I stole them. I'm sorry but I'm being punished for my crime."

Later the general sat again in the governor's office.

"Amazing," he said. "You've got one hundred and one innocent men here – except for that Jacob Fischer. He's obviously in the wrong place. Set him free at once."

Notes

Follow up themes: excuses; truth; rewards.

This Jewish story could be used at the time of the Jewish Festival of Yom Kippur. This Day of Atonement is one of fasting and praying for forgiveness and the story could be used in connection with two such features – 'saving life' (pikuach nefesh) and 'mending the world' (tikum olam).

Yom Kippur comes nine days after the Jewish New Year Autumn Festival of Rosh Hashanah.

The closing prayer for this assembly might be based on past of the old Jewish prayer from Psalm 12:

Dear God, Please forgive me for the sinful things I have done in my life and help me always to be ready to make a new start. Amen.

99
All for one
(Wesak)

This Buddhist story emphasises the benefits of having friends who are prepared to help in time of need.

"I'm caught! I'm caught!"

The antelope's voice rang out through the forest as the leather noose of the trap tightened round him.

"I'm caught!"

Deep in the forest the tortoise and the woodpecker heard the cry. They were the antelope's closest friends.

"Quick," said the woodpecker, "our friend needs help."

When they found the trapped antelope the woodpecker spoke again.

"Don't worry my friend, we'll soon have you free. Tortoise – you start gnawing those leather bonds and I'll go and make sure the hunter does not come."

For hours the tortoise gnawed at the thongs until his teeth and gums ached. Meanwhile the woodpecker found the hunter's hut and every time he came out of the door she drove him back by flapping her wings in his face. Finally she could do it no more and, seizing a huge knife, the hunter surged through the wood to where the antelope was trapped. The woodpecker flew ahead of him.

"He's coming, he's coming!" she cried out.

Hearing this the antelope threw his weight against the weakened bonds and broke free. At once he fled into the trees. The tortoise however was exhausted and just lay there gasping as the hunter burst into the clearing.

Seeing that the antelope had escaped, and instantly realising how it had done so the hunter let out a cry of rage.

"You!" he snarled at the tortoise. "Well, you'll pay for this!"

So saying he hauled the tortoise into a sack and tied the neck tightly.

Now the antelope, once hidden in the trees, had turned to see what had happened to the tortoise.

"I must help," he thought, and immediately started crashing about in the forest.

Hearing the noise the hunter looked up and saw the antelope, who was pretending to be hurt.

"Aah!" cried the hunter. "It won't take me long to catch you!"

So saying he set off in chase of the antelope – who just kept ahead of him until they were deep in the forest. Then, throwing off his pretended limp, the antelope leapt out of sight and raced back to where the tortoise lay in the sack.

"We'll soon have you out of there," cried the antelope, ripping the sack open. Overhead the woodpecker circled, keeping watch. Soon the tortoise was free.

"Now my friends thank you for saving me," said the antelope. "That hunter will soon be back so I suggest we hide in another part of the forest until he has gone altogether."

This they did, and remained happy and friends, long after the hunter had moved on.

Notes

Follow up themes: friendship; sticking together.

This Buddhist story is from the *Jataka*, which is the 'birth story' of the Buddha and contains accounts of his previous lives. In this tale the Buddha has assumed the form of the antelope. This assembly could be used for the festival occasion of Wesak, the celebration of the date on which the birth, Enlightenment and death of the Buddha all took place. With regard to this a check of the annual dates of religious festivals for the current year would be necessary, but Wesak is a full moon festival in early summer in Western calendars.

Concluding prayer:

Let us give thanks this morning for friends and the pleasure, fun, help and support they give us. Let us pray that each of us might always be considered a good friend. Amen.

100
Who can help you?
(Eid-ul-Fitr)

We all feel guilty about something we have done in our lives. In this morning's story a man who felt guilty was nearly driven to a terrible deed.

Rachid was angry.

"That Muhammad," he thought, "I hate him. How dare he tell us we should worship only one God called Allah. And the way he gives his money away and frees slaves – it's enough to put a man out of business."

Now the real secret of Rachid's anger was that he felt guilty. He never gave any money away, he never helped others and he wasn't sure why he worshipped several gods.

"If I got rid of Muhammad everything would be all right again," thought Rachid bitterly.

He looked round him. The great camel caravan was resting on its journey through the desert. A blazing sun shone down and everyone was taking a siesta before continuing the journey when it got cooler.

Rachid reached for his sword and stealthily crept over to the shade where Muhammad slept. Nearer and nearer he got until, the point of his sword was pressed against the sleeping man's throat.

"Now," he hissed in Muhammad's ear, "before I kill you, tell me who can save you?"

Muhammad woke instantly and, without a flicker of fear, answered immediately.

"You won't kill me, Rachid," he said quietly, "because Allah will save me."

Expecting Muhammad to be terrified, Rachid was confused by his response. Seeing his confusion Muhammad wrenched the sword from his enemy's grip and, leaping to his feet, pressed its blade against Rachid's throat.

"Now," he whispered, "who can save you?"

"Only you," gasped the frightened Rachid, "only you."

"And of course I will," replied Muhammad, "but remember only do unto others what you would like them to do to you."

After this incident Rachid thought a lot about what Muhammad had said and so he became a Muslim too and followed Muhammad's teachings.

Notes

Follow up themes: learning lessons; thinking before we act.

The Muslim festival of Eid-ul-Fitr celebrates the end of the monthly fast of Ramadan. (Consult current *Calendar of Religious Festivals* for annual dates of Muslim Festivals.) Eid-ul-Fitr is probably the Muslim festival which is enjoyably celebrated more than any other. It can last for three days in Muslim countries, but celebrations are usually restricted to one day amongst Muslims in Britain.

Concluding prayer:

Let us pray this morning for wisdom in thinking before we act hastily. Let us remember that a harsh word cannot be taken back, and an unkind deed can give us much sorrow. Let us always try to behave to other people as we would like them to behave to us. Amen.